Colleen;

May you enjoy my
poems as you enjoy your
stay in TorC and The New Mexico
State Veterans Home

Stan

TROTH AND RAPTURE

TROTH AND RAPTURE

400 Sonnets

Stanley Paul Thompson

Mercury HeartLink
www.heartlink.com

Troth & Rapture — 400 Sonnets

Erratum: *Troth and Rapture:400 Sonnets*

The use of old middle English got mixed up in poem number 4. In the listing of poems and of the title of *A Foolish Yong Rogue—4* is correct, but to correspond to the first line of the couplet; Darling Peter you're a foolish young rogue it should read 'yong rogue'. Both words mean basically the same, however I do wish to be consistent.

Stanley Paul Thompson, Author and Poet

INTERLUDE OF LOVE

RESUME ALPHABETICAL LISTING

ACKNOWLEDGMENTS

These are the people that have helped me understand the complexities of writing good poems; unsung heroes, I honor them. They are poets who, once a month on a Sunday afternoon, bring their original poetry to recite in Truth or Consequences, New Mexico. A more jovial crowd I would be hard pressed to assemble. There is no rancor, no hoots and hollers, no getting up and storming out; these poets respect each and every one to the poems read. I salute them all.

But I would be remiss if I didn't give full credit to my wife and companion, Karen; she has been the 'push' behind this tome of 400 sonnets and without her I may never had found the time to submit these sonnets for publication. To her instead of a salute I give a heartfelt hug.

INTRODUCTION

Since publishing my first book, *Sonnets of Life Well Spent*, I have written over 3500 poems, of these, near 1000 are sonnets. Not wishing to duplicate those published beforehand, I had from over 850 to choose these 400 sonnets that are in this tome. This was no simple task, as I had to re-read all of them and then select what I felt were representative poem themes.

My poems are almost exclusively written in the format of Shakespeare. Many of these read as if one in the sixteenth or seventeenth century had sat and penned sonnets of that period. Those I hope add flavor to those wanting a feel of the Renaissance Period.

As is the prerogative of poets, I have used words that today are not in vogue, being supplanted by modern English usage. Still, I feel they are words that convey a deeper meaning. For instance, I have used both settling and setting to the sun's demise in the west; the former to suggest a softer movement, while the latter to be thus said and done.
I have also rescued the word gay and have used it in the way it was meant; namely, happily excited, as Merriam-Webster's Collegiate Dictionary points out.

When you read my sonnets I want you to have a dictionary at your elbow, or if you have a computer or similar means, those will suffice. Then when a word mystifies, look it up so you understand the context in which it was used. This tome is not meant to be read in a day, a week, or even in a month. I suspect that a few each night will keep you guessing as to what each means. Bear in mind that in a number of my sonnets you will never guess what I was talking about; those you will have to dream as to their meaning.

There are two special groups of poems; *Three Poems on Love and Ode to the French Revolution (A love story-13 sonnets)*. They all are in the order in which I have written them and are placed alphabetically in the L section under love. In the third of the Three Poems on Love, *Taken When Let*, I use the phrase, cone-shaped device to speak. I refer you to search for

Rudy Vallee and the way he projected his singing voice. In the *Ode to the French Revolution* I had originally written twelve sonnets but then later I realized that there might be questions as to the ending of the twelfth sonnet, so to answer any questions I added *But I Like My Ending*.

I have been blessed in knowing fabulous women throughout my life and there are sonnets which speak to these relationships throughout the tome. In all of these relationships I have absolutely no regrets. There is one now that is my wife, and she has been a driving force in pushing me to publish these sonnets. In her reading of all the nearly 850 sonnets she has done a yeoman's job. Very few wives would have done this without throwing up their hands and saying; enough!

One of the sonnets in this tome is the following:

Stands Me Well in Stature

I have tried poems of a different nature
But I write less of verse without rhyming
As so many do with éclat I'm sure
That my absence even of prose, nothing

For my notice is in sonnets I write
Of love, romance, even of tales once told
Perhaps venture of verse as to incite
In my readers more of mystique of old

Ah, but of love I choose to write sonnets
In the style of Shakespeare; he's my master
So I plead to forgive my use of its
Style, so olde of England's words and grammar

Let me then pen my poems most of structure
As rhymed meter stands me well in stature

This sonnet expresses what I have written, and more likely, better than I could write in this introduction.

This book is dedicated to all the women I have encountered through my life's adventure. They have been special to me in their own way and I have gained love and happiness from each one.

TROTH AND RAPTURE

A Fair Venus

Oh tis lovely; her face in bright sunshine
The glint off her forehead; ah that is fair
And when she squints is she teasing a sign
Such am I now smitten; I'll not unswear

She walks through my vision, filling it whole
I am silenced with the beauty I see
My love goes with the wind yet I cajole
But she remains in my eyesight scarcely

Then in trailing are her fairies and sprites
Likely they will protect her from all harm
I must catch them before the sun twilights
As in dark my presence may cause alarm

This a body that P. Rubens would paint
A fair Venus my gods let me anoint

A FEW ITEMS SOLD

Twas a wild night, the Black and White affair
A fire had torched the roof away and left
Standing bare walls festooned with lights gayer
This lent the art present for guests to sift

A rock band played music which gave aura
As red shoes with green toes vied with others
There be judged the zany costume they wore
As the vendor in black and white dress lures

The wind for a while gave fits to art shown
And while blackouts caused some moments of doubt
More light was brought in which stifled the moan
As some flashlights were seen and then put out

So how did they judge the event en masse
A few items sold but most gave it a pass

A FIRM STANCE STOOD

Twinkie comes to head butt my lap table
Then she settles against my leg to rest
She's all alert as some thunder's able
To fire off a bolt of lightning guessed

Celtic Woman playing while I write this
I've got four disks, so that's about three hours
Right up to near midnight as comes sleeps bliss
And three more poems as when it rain it pours

I think that this Friday morn I'll take Mike
And we'll go to Happy Belly Deli
He with his sketch pad and me with delight
To be in the outdoors; comfy feely

I can see I'm in a pretty good mood
I've sloughed off my problems, a firm stance stood

A Foolish Yong Rogue

I come to charm you faire maiden, a bint
You will note my accouterments I take
To woo you and take one as did Peer Gynt
For I'm of vile pretense as my name sake

You scare not as Peer Gynt, I see your bluff
Of such bluster and you do so swagger
Did you learn that from Don Juan, if so, guff
What I will do is call your marm; tell her

Oh sweet Sally, you have waited so long
And my ventures have seen me less gallant
But I have tales to speak of that prolong
My vast journey, dare I speak of valiant

Darling Peter you're a foolish young rogue
I see you for what you are, out of vogue

A Fresh New Start

With each mile I feel my heart is rending
As we move more apart; then help me grow
Reverse this most awful feeling, ending
Heartache, stopping the pain, making it go

And why should I help you poet who plies
Takes of love and gives back nothing worthwhile
For you do well without my help of lies
I might even think you relish your style

But you mistake my cry for help pleading
Tis of her I ask for aid in healing
So be gone now my call at last leading
To a tranquil finis, fondest feeling

I shall stop and call her, appease my heart
Then on morrow begin a fresh new start

A GIFT OF CAKE

How can I now explain what you have sensed
That I will be sailing away come morn
Once more I will explore, then chart what can'st
Have been done on my last voyage foreign

My dear I make promise that this my third
Of trips to the new world will be my last
And thus will be able to write in word
Of Cook's success of these mappings so vast

Liz please explain thus to our three children
As they all want me home safely and sound
Such pain you have borne with three now deaden
Pray that no more leave us, their deaths to hound

I have on good advice agreed to make
The King of all Hawaii a gift of cake

A GOLD MEDAL WINNER

It was your blithe smile that Stan most fancies
He would look at you and know, here comes fun
With those huge lensed glasses, those eyes he sees
And dreams of gay outings under the sun

For you were his partner Pat, more perhaps
As you raised the family while he was gone
And took care of finance while he took naps
A true frontier woman if there was one

You were charming; could play hostess when called
And rare were you tipsy like he might be
But that held charm too, his antics recalled
For he was the paycheck, life made easy

I would rate this marriage quite high on points
A gold medal winner if one anoints

A Jewel Was Found

From this very ground a jewel was found
Of such beauty were its sparkles beheld
That when first viewed all sorts of men confound
Then whence came this omen that men's soul's meld

They knocked at my castle, my home to me
Come out sir, we command at this moment
I said come in; I hold secrets fastly
So ask not of jewel or its portent

They read me my rights, or wrongs done crafty
Under arrest, I spoke not a sound then
In jail I had coffee, my cell drafty
Then in morn my bail paid, no ride given

A long trip back to my home sans taxi
Would you know they thought the jewel waxy

A Job Would Be Offered

That first winter would test hard their mettle
Unless the late comers found warm shelter
With friends or near family to share of victual
Many would starve; be found frozen later

But most were quite hardy; of stock Norsk wed
And if kept dry, disease might just pass by
Yet in crowded cities rooms were sordid
With small pox and measles; the deaths ran high

Still life was no worse than Norway before
The same cold, lack of food; utter despair
But a promise that in springtime, much more
For the taking; farms wanted repair

If you had a trade, say working with wood
A job would be offered; good work then stood

A Kiss of Nubbles

Letting all of my sorrow be flushed out
This my cleansing of those darkened topics
I do this to remove bad thoughts that doubt;
Artists do this when they paint myopic's

Then when I am purified, I resume
As freshness enters my mind and I write
Poems that acclaim the good life; not of doom
But of sonnets which help lovers unite

Oh, write of the moon and those sparkling stars
Of night's stillness when objects are ashen
Then draw your partner close; hear the guitars
That plays music of romance and passion

This then of my letting go of troubles
To be replaced with a kiss of nubbles

A Lifetime That's Fulfilled

This poet's life is of but finite length
For then one day no more poetry rife
But till that fateful time I write with strength
And give little nod to my after life

Your gift to me is to prod my writing
To cheer my sad moods, to temper manic
To give of your love, what ever's fitting
And I'll return epic poems eurhythmic

I wish you to help me with publishing
To help select my poems that are most good
Then to read them carefully; polishing
Each phrase, each rhyme so they are understood

Then we can have a lifetime that's fulfilled
With poems of note, their values now instilled

A Love Tune Symphonic

Come run with me, tis a dance I'm taking
To soothe aching limbs and broken heartstrings
Come, you'll be most welcome and no faking
We have enough of these; sourness there brings

The dance is quite simple; and fools take part
So do not now worry; come one, come all
We have been there before; some at the start
It's like a waltz; twirling about; a brawl

Oh we mingle and some even press lips
But those are the ones that have a problem
The rest, not you, of more abstruse courtships
Happen to have love that has grown tiresome

But there is hope and post hoc a tonic
It is music, a love tune symphonic

A MOST HUMBLE POET

Hark now I pray am I worthy seeking
Doth my poem here entrance you with rapture
For if it does consider me worth keeping
As I'll write my songs of love to capture

But if you then avoid my true advances
And deem my words most weak, even specious
Then to a cave to live like Saint Francis
There to think that I might write less cautious

Then let my sonnet as Sisyphus soar
Ever trying to reach the height of love
As was said; to fill a man's heart, in lore
Ne'er treacherous the ebb and flow thereof

In truth I pray you will accept me as
A most humble poet yet amorous

A Norseman's Lad Who Loves You

I want to tell you that my love reaches
The far corners of that world you habit
Thick walls cannot hide, for my love breaches
Even castle dungeon of stone's jacket

And then when it touches you; oh so mellow
Like the dew of Fairies; full of magic
You'll think only of this poet fellow
Who pens his love sonnets sometimes Orphic

That I send this to you from far off land
Shows my resolve; that this love will perdure
I will comfort you and give of my hand
My grip gentle, yet strong so you'll be sure

I am but a Norseman's lad who loves you
Who will fight trolls if need be to rescue

A Park to Camp In

How many trees do you suppose there are
Billions, probably trillions; maybe there's more
Like blades of grass, who cares, they're everywhere
Should make Greenie's happy, even Al Gore

From my RV window I count sixty
But there are many times more in background
I haven't seen Squirrels; are they hungry
Parks are good hang-out spots; are Bears around

Probably some Deer, Skunks and a sly Raccoon
And where are the birds; I saw a Robin
But that was all; perhaps they're here at noon
Just now heard a peep, peep; someone's bobbin

Give me a park to camp in and I'll stay
They are peaceful and don't cost much per day

A Road Different

I have this new feeling; a road different
That I need to herald my poems in print
And get my name known by writing current
Events about my town; news print I'll mint

There is a real yearning for things refined
Art, music, plays, movies and poetry
To go along with the hot springs; combined
With a hot soak, my love poems; coquetry

I've made contact with a woman that might
Agree to print a poem about this town
Its peoples and events; to give starlight
To my writings, to make me then renown

So I'll send three or four short poems; bestir
Like Keats and the others, my poems to her

A Tear I Detect

Perhaps you were precise in my going
As the travel trailer lacks in comfort
And with my cat you won't find her moaning
Rather we're like pilot and co–pilot

I am used to small spaces to live in
And like the soft snugness of my pillows
As for showers, there are buildings near then
Where I can use all the water allows

And if I snore; I said if, didn't I
Then my pet cat Twinkie hasn't complained
And if she mews, then I won't bat an eye
We've lived as dear partners as I've explained

No, your letting me go now seems correct
Ah...and is that then a tear I detect

A Two College Town

I must have been tired for I slept deeply
Dreams, then long passed by of memories ago
Flashed through my mind, a few made me weeply
In the morn my pillow was damp as though

This find day, as coolness becomes the air
I will complete what I promised to do
To find here then closure of love's despair
That was squandered in youth, telling words true

Have I had the success that I hoped here
Well, time will tell for it mightn't show of
But I do have projects in mind with her
To write my poems of her paintings of love

I have finished this poem now in Northfield
A two college town that fits as I've quilled

A Wave Passing

She looked askance at me; of little means
He will make a barmaid happy perhaps
But for you my precious he's not what seems
For love comes in all flavors; this one's schnapps

Tis true my sweet; what she saith not absurd
I offer what the Reynard fox gives thereof
To his Vixen fox; what the Hummingbird
Presents to the fertile flower; it's called love

Were it not for your friends, all overspent
And the grand manner to which accustomed
You and I wouldst be happy and content
A night at the pub; ne'er to be lonesome'd

But, let us still be friends; a wave passing
And perhaps in your heart what you're missing

−ABLE IS AND −IBLE

For words that have ending; −ible use care
As its Latin words use only I'll state
Does that mean you must know Latin to fare
No, if you drop −ible, then no word spate

There are some words that void this rule of thumb
So it is not out−and−out a precept
Learn their number; say two hundred will come
Best just recall those ones listed as apt

Now the rest are −able; could be Latin
But most likely modern usage is known
Drop the −able and a word you see then
Loaning with end; −able, becomes just loan

There are words that are not endings per se
−able is and −ible; Bible no way

ACT AS LIFEGUARDS

Don't quell my soul, but let me rile away
Writing what's felt; desires of the lonely
Those that need help along their own byway
Travelers of these side roads they've known only

There is little that this sonnet can do
Other than to condole where there is need
Still I must try while some attempt, argue;
All that's required is that the State spoon-feed

I'm a watchdog; keeping options open
That one's life is sacred; not to be ruled
By do-gooders saying; this way's golden
And then soothing words made, they are cajoled

So join with me; this fight condign as bards
And help the down-trodden; act as lifeguards

Ah, There Is Warmth Again

I felt her there beside, the warmth welcome
But then I moved and she rose up and left
Was I wrong, just nothing my dreams outcome
Was it Twinkie or just a light wind waft

No, I shook that away and tried to sleep
Silly of my pretend that sensed her near
But I have heard murmurs, whispers that seep
Into my mind, that's a problem I fear

And I shant find pennies now strewn about
Nor strange creaking of floor boards at midnight
I'll put these thoughts away, let mice come out
Critters that prowl throughout the house and fight

Ah, there is warmth again, I feel the heat
Perhaps it is Twinkie now by my feet

ALL ABOUT HAVING DISPORTS

Have I gone on these trips to help forget
Driving keeps my mind on the road focused
Akin to my sailing off toward sunset
Hoping I can gen up hocus–pocussed

I'll let onto a big secret right now
Because this trip hasn't helped as I planned
Sure there were times when I didn't avow
But I stumbled over thoughts that were banned

So what is the answer; it's not better
I could lay it on God's doorstep to solve
Would he suggest some sort of fetter
That would keep my thoughts of her to dissolve

Perhaps I have gotten what God purports
That life is all about having disports

All of Past is Silence

If I were to be a playwright; let's see
Wouldst be drama of verse or prose certain
Written as a burlesque; comic it be
Liken to one of the Shakespeare's pertain

On the other hand, thus sad, one of tragic
And if my own then most sorely written
No, I find this woeful and no magic
Could come of my demise, my heart bitten

A third option might then mimic history
Present in time format, coming of age
Thus not rule out mine own lifetime story
Enlarge on poem, Ode to Stan, a barrage

If I should take this path, I ask guidance
For once began all of past is silence

ALL OUR CARES BEGONE OF IT

This night such joy I find writing poems of
Let not word and phrase and rhyme speak despairs
For I'm captured as you hold me near love
And my sonnet becomes muted whispers

Then hush I say as I embrace with you
My arms around, pressing you close, now sure
As I meet your lips with mine, fresh like dew
To taste of sweet nectar, oh such rapture

Then let us walk here with starlight only
I wrap my coat around your bare shoulder
Then you rest your arm in mine there fondly
As we now walk faster, the air colder

Such is love then inscribed in my sonnet
As we let all our cares begone of it

Allow Then This Call

To hear your voice is like the soft breeze blown
That now refreshes the air stagnant of loss
Ah, tis cool this breath for that I have known
Before when my lips to kiss came across

Yet I would cherish but a light caress
Of your finger tips on my cheek; this touch
Reminds of those moments we'd coalesce
Yet which I so foolish of mind debouch

All my waking hours and of sleep; there too
You have entered my thoughts; I am immured
In these dream–like states that I then bestrew
As the pain grips my heart once so cocksure'd

Allow then this call for I do languish
I beg of a word. A phrase you'd lavish

Always Pleasing Her Feed

Cool and cloudy, fall is upon us now
So a sip of coffee feels warm inside
Couple that with a Bran muffin and wow
I'm now ready to write sonnets aside

Upstairs above Eastman's, Grandma Thompson
Had her rooms, first in back, then much later
In front where I'd watch the change in season
By the lights and décor; storefront dater

On my way from high school I would stop by
Anna would put cookies and milk for treat
And we would talk about my life she'd pry
Was I singing; just small tit–bits of greet

Anna's coffee had grounds so she would read
Of my fortune, always pleasing her feed

Always the Man Must Ask

Have you ever sat quite alone and thought
About things that happened and why they did
Trying to put vis–à–vis her varied naughts
To your offers and why always low bid

Tis these matters that once confuse and deign
For no logic can be found her retort
As she simply says, I need not explain
And you wouldn't percept the scent of Port

Low bid and Port, is this scandal inferred
For I am most honest, she knows full well
I'll ask her now, perhaps I have deferred
This blunt exchange, but my darling tis hell

Always the man must ask, but then accede
To her wishes or of good health you cede

Always the Same Sunday

Does it now feel different, this place of old
Can I close my eyes and see me standing
At the bus stop, Fourth and Central, quite cold
As I await my ride, homeward landing

When the weather was nice I walked Ravine
Turned north on Sixth Ave, then right on Third Street
Then straight ahead Shumway, the bus leaving
I wave as it passes onto Deaf School's beat

The top of the world or so it seemed then
High towards the bluffs across the Straight River
Dad would coast down Ravine to save gas when
World War rations made gas hard to secure

The time getting late I rush home hungry
Supper at six, always the same Sunday

AMOROUS HINTS IN DESIGN

Oh tis now that you have aroused me well
Am I to lay here as unspoiled my Lord
Then take me to wonders known; a bombshell
You shall ignite; certain to strike a chord

You read your lines quite well; do you practice
Only when I find a willing partner,
One that has no remorse wishing to kiss
And thank god that is rare after dinner

In that case I propose that we rehearse
A more charming place would be my abode
Please don't think that I would even coerce
A fond kiss; still my lines might heat; explode

When of practice, look then beyond each line
See if there are amorous hints in design

AND ALL THE KINGS MEN

When you open up your secrets held fast
You are feeling much more secure in love
And he sees you naked; your shields now cast
Aside; there you stand now open; thought of

When she sees you in the raw; not shaven
Being at a loss of witty remarks
Wonder what had happened to that goal driven
Poet who made sonnets of love has sparks

Both now are purged of hurt; thank God for it
And can move on; they're free from the past's toll
I say let them enjoy this fine respite
For they have earned marriage of minds and soul

Now pass the word; true love has now burst forth
And all the King's men can't change what its worth

AND I ASK; WHERE ARE YOU

I did not stir from home this warm Sunday
Little things to do kept my mind busy
Watered my trees, fed the birds their buffet
Took no nap, wrote poems till I felt drowsy

And now I'm on number five of my six
Still I feel I just might write more than that
Finish my notebook; write more of metrics
Then take a break and quickly feed my cat

There'll be no call tonight; I miss them so
But you'll be at Mira's with her children
And the hours of nine will pass in shadow
You're tired body soon to bed I reckon

Next comes Monday and I start that anew
No wake–up call and I ask; where are you

AND I'M JUST HAPPY WRITING

We don't know much about Shakespeare's moments
Those late at night sessions when his pen flew
Did he write at his desk or recumbent
Wouldst there be a flagon of wine there too

In two hundred years I want no question
Those arm chair scholar's telling; he's like this
When they wouldn't have a clue to fashion
So I'll leave some clues; faceless none–the–less

I write on the couch, while eating sometime
But mostly sprawled on my bed with Twinkie
That's my cat and I sleep in the nude prime
It gets hot in New Mexico you see

And I'm just happy writing about her
My Norwegian Princess; painter; lover

And Like Darnay Ask

Tonight I saw "A Tale of Two Cities"
Dickens classic story of one's last breath
For he gives the utmost as he pities
The wife and child while her Darnay waits death

And I marvel at what Carton has done
I am heedful of what true love entails
That the deepest feelings can then be gone
When one gives up his claim to life and pales

Dickens calls forth inner strength from his men
That what they give is more priceless by far
Than what they could have just taken of then
So my heart goes out to Carton's dolor

Could it be then that God's given us life
And like Darnay, ask that you be my wife

AND SAFE WITHIN MY EAR

Her song is in my mind I dare not pause
To leave a note unsung, to hear at last
Then shall I write of love for it may cause
My heart to break this love that was in past

I shall not leave this tune to go away
The voice I hear dulcet, a smile now comes
And cares I'd fret are lost, they will not stay
I am then en rapport, my heart now hums

What strange things doth bother this mind of mine
Am I possessed, cursed; do Elfin's tarry
Then set traps that harass for I opine
That for spite my love of her they bury

But I will fool them well; feign sound asleep
And safe within my ear her voice I'll keep

And So I Sped

I missed you the moment I left your door
I thought about should I return again
But that would make goodbye harder once more
So I promised to call your cell phone then

I'm glad you packed my lunch; it served me well
Snacking while I'm driving; a go getter
Cause a burger and fries is fat count hell
While an apple and some cheese better

I left at six; arrived Liberal at nine
Nearly made nine hundred miles now today
A good rest in Super Eight, then I'll dine
With their breakfast at six; onward, I say

Well the best plans are fraught to change and did
I left at three–thirty, and so I sped

And the Tale is Complete

All my life I have worked to make my goal
And Sir, nothing will now deter my aim
Even true love I cried; foolish your role
She then replied, this love is not my game

My heart was then shattered; I thought I'd die
That love was ranked second; how could this be
She'll change her mind; of love she can't deny
I'll wait her out; in time I'll claim victory

But then time heals the heart sullen and ill
And young love is tempted once more to roam
And the girl he once knew; no more the thrill
And of course he had no recourse of poem

Now I can look back and smile at my fate
As the tale is complete rather than late

And Thoughts of His Capture

Then guide me home swiftly; you of west wind
Your Greek name is Zephyrus; Cupid's right hand
I need you now; Psyche, you must rescind
Let fair Cupid bring her to his own land

Now that I have your full notice; heed well
There are ships that pursue; gaining they be
I ask for much blowing; there to propel
My ship and crew safely across the sea

I am Aeneas, Trojan Prince of Troy
Hero of the poet Virgil in time
These Greeks that now follow; do not be coy
I am the one sonnets record in rhyme

And with this gods breath the distance improved
And thoughts of his capture were then removed

And Watch the Sun Settling

When I'm wistful my thoughts harken to you
For you have told me that love comes slowly
Trickling as does melting snow drifts into
My heart; thus filled once more; love's then wholly

Such joy this brings knowing that you are mine
As I am yours in most wondrous amour
No more pensive; for my yearnings of thine
Have been fulfilled; I am complete, secure

Like two Eagles, flying now side–by–side
Solo, yet we're paired like the Blue Angels
Matching every twist and turn, we abide
In these per'lous events as love's equals

When our day is finished we'll sit on high
And watch the sun settling in the west sky

And What Were the Outcomes

I want you to share in these my memories
When at night I would fly, my thoughts there true
When the blackness complete when flown the seas
And my wingman held close beneath my view

There is no light except cockpits red glow
And his dim lights hardly seen from afar
I'd pass the time humming a tune I know
Flexing my legs, checking switches for war

Then straight ahead blue lights like of Woading
Powerhouse this is Red Wing, do you read me
I will Roger him, state my bomb loading
You are cleared to drop on flares when ready

As I turn my Skyhawk, blackness welcomes
Once more to hum and what were the outcomes

AND WON SANCTUARY

The power of love that puts me near you
That brings your image when I close my eyes
Is it dreaming when you play peekaboo
Teasing me, then on tiptoes kiss goodbyes

And this force which holds my heart of ransom
Be it strong; I want to be your prisoner
Even the pain of torture I welcome
Shouting my love for you, my questioner

When I'm dragged, broken to my prison cell
And thrown face down on the cold cobblestones
I can still hear the song of Philomel
That sound kings have paid with gold, soothes my groans

Mighty are my thoughts now in reverie
I've suffered love and won sanctuary

And Yet is Blind

I can recall walking along the shore
And there seeing water boils made by fish
Spots on a clear surface to underscore
That there beneath fish are feeding lavish

But if there are waves then these boils aren't seen
But the feeding still goes on underneath
And those that walk the shore can't see the scene
But rest assured there are some hungry teeth

So too are strong feelings seen and hidden
Like surface boils, they appear then vanish
And in everyday events forbidden
But neath the surface these ardors languish

The mind doth comprehend what God intends
And yet is blind to those that he suspends

ART IS LONG, LIFE IS SHORT

I have given what has been asked of us
To paint of life so bold yet it bothers
The Pope and his henchmen here most grievous
That they've jailed me along with some others

This morn I was tortured, asked to confess
That my art was Demon inspired, in fact
I have refused and thus await distress
Which I'm told is given in print redact

I fear not my fate, yet lament my life
To be shortened and not able to draw
My last series that wouldst depict the strife
Of all artists here, that paints life as raw

I will gladly offer my life in this
Latin prayer; *ars longa vita brevis*

Ars longa vita brevis – Art is long, life is short

As His Hormones Still are Active

Oh I'm so blessed, like a schoolboy in love
That I would kiss your hands and kiss your toes
Someone stop me before I kiss more of
My mind is numb, where then this goes, who knows

Slow down and catch your breath, you need not run
The girls won't turn away, they're quite docile
And known to flirt, even rumored of fun
Put a hold on urges, they won't wrestle

You might want to take them flowers; a Rose
Would be nice, a dozen even better
With a box of candy, dandy suppose
There, you're set, all things calmed down go–getter

Putting the brakes on this poet is hard
As his hormones still are active, this bard

As His Sonnet in Form

To speak of love, to feel of love; rapture
For there are no feelings greater in life
Thus it is with me that you must lecture
That with patience may come rewards of wife

And should our lives ne'er join then en rapport
Then I shall still worship you till life's end
And I pray those most dear see our love for
What it means to us and shun not as friend

These brief moments that we're apart wear me
My mind cannot condense them to nothing
And at night when I am writing I see
There the image of my love beseeching

Tis then Shakespeare in whom I seek refuge
As his sonnets in form allow this nudge

As I Search For Your Love

Do you love less now that I've gone away
Has the memory faded of those months spent
In such blissful rapture on your duvet
When in honest whispers said love's intent

It is ard'ous for me to think that love
Could go for naught; almost in an instant
Maybe I failed in that; what was said of
Marriage shouldn't have; I now wish I hadn't

I tried hard to be a special friend too
But my heart is not in sync with my brain
And it sends my mind mixed signals, askew
All–in–all this becomes for me insane

I am trying; God knows of my struggles
As I search for your love in the rubbles

As They're Frosting on Cake

Love came early when I heard your sweet voice
Waking up; your sleepy hello just a
Pleasant preview of things to come that's nice
Did you stretch and purr with my wake today

Of course I can only guess what you do
But I know a smile must be on your face
As you think it's minutes early; so true
And when waking did you pretend efface

I do treasure these calls early morning
Heavens, I must include calls made at night
Was I to then compare; well a warning
Sound might prompt me to tread careful this write

I shall simply state that all calls I make
Are most wondrous as they're frosting on cake

As We Need to Rehearse

Where are these doubts that plague sleepless my nights
Come out and show yourselves; hide not from me
I am not then afraid, I'll take on fights
And will battle each and all that there be

Oh you secrete well my bane of skepsis
Coming out to haunt me when I'm pensive
You must watch me closely; art thou menseless
A lout dear sir making me thus tensive

Wait, stop; this play is not about tension
It is supposed to be debate most fierce
You, get me the playwright; schedule at one
He will have to rewrite; cash from my purse

Do you want the actors to come back too
As we need to rehearse the play now through

At Her Beck and Call

I've said that love comes in different sizes
For some that means a show and tell posture
But for others it shows diverse guises;
You take your pick; its wash and wear rapture

This year I've picked a more youthful outfit
To prove that I'm not a fuddy–duddy
I have to say this look becomes a hit,
My pulse quickens and my color's ruddy

My wife she likes to buy those hand–me–downs
And I admit she does often bewitch
In hues of reds, yellows, greens, blues and browns
A most charming woman; she fits my niche

I am what one calls; a one–size fits all
Ready then to be at her beck and call

Be Most Gallant

If one's stubborn or say mulish of thought
There is needed tact to reverse this trait
While some may say well voiced debate be brought
I will lay with patience, let rest this wait

Say one propose of love and finds it no
If you persist then she girds her defense
And all further pleadings will find more woe
Thus she's entrenched to soon mount her offense

Let us repeat; she's said no to your ask
You might then pause...then say adieu and leave
She will ponder all night; you might just bask
Then in a week call her, date her, don't grieve

Now she will think, will he ask me again
Be most gallant, let love restart, begin

Be Then Honest in Thought

In talks of love I hear your voice invite
Am I dreaming, will I awake to see
You close by me, your arms around me tight
And I'll answer; yes my dear that will be

We both have these packets of should I tell
Silly thoughts that have no meaning to us
Friendships even, ones that appear as well
But love, we have lived far apart so shush

I will tell you; forget about the past
These are memories that must now lay dormant
To let these now linger opens a vast
Amount of just nothings, plainly we shant

Then say we trust our hearts, forget the rest
Be then honest in thought, I know that's best

BEING THE DON IS TIRING

Are you looking at me, speaking to me
If so, then state your case or be off then
My times precious and times money you see
Are you asking for more cat food my friend

Quit you're staring, I can't blink, no eyelid
And that mark near my nose; let's just say nice
If I told you I'd have to kill you kid
So back off some or your paws in a vice

Next please; no need to rub my nose either
What's that you say, that fat kittens my sire
Get-out-a-here, he's got no tail beater
And you don't look au fait; go or I'll fire

Being the Don is tiring but what the heck
Someone's got to do it; at call and beck

Better Then They're Unsaid

From the foot of my bed she stared; impish
Come hither girl, let not my gruff face warn
Come now and sit here beside; don't languish
I'm your grandsire and you, my Capricorn

Born on Christ's Day to my eldest daughter
God rest her soul; and now a grown woman
I've made inquiries of this young writer
A poet is he not, and not common

He is the first son of a Duke, my Lord
And he writes poems and odes that lift my heart
Why in London he's just won an award
I love him so deeply, this bard upstart

So my child I shall give blessing to wed
Should some then voice; better then they're unsaid

BEWARE OF THE PIRATE

There through her veil I did see of beauty
Whose dark eyes of passion arouse a thrill
Was that a smile too I see; such booty
That I've taken cannot compare; as nil

Let me present my case; jewels I offer
You do not seem alarmed; might you explain
I've seen you; what is the name you proffer
It's not Blue Beard; perhaps it is Fonteyn

Then why offer me gems; were they plunder
But you too would steal my heart in exchange
So I see no reason why you wonder
As this is an even barter arrange

Beware of the pirate who steals your heart
For it takes more than a veil to outsmart

Beyond the Pale

I did not mean any harm, please believe
Though you've been caught like a Moth in a net
You were always free, that I shant deceive
And with time you grew to love me, dammit

Was it the glint of my eyes that bewitched
Did it thither to my nest then drawing
Or did perfume so sweet bring you beseeched
For I'd accept then this premise knowing

There were bounds to explain; something forgot
Then soon added for no one is perfect
Fences you'd called them, I'd say no they're not
More like the lines between countries affect

I am sorry that this seemed like a jail
But no way could you go beyond the pale

Both of Love Healings

Then a flood of memories infused my heart
When I heard your voice say; yes it's Anne–Marit
I paused, it seemed aeons before I start
Then in whispers, my name I did impart

And you were so gracious; what else expect
Did you ever think of me with favor
I don't know of course, why I should suspect
That a campus romance invite savor

Was my motive made clear, to send my book
Or did you sense something more in my tone
As I recall even the least we took
Such were my fond memories that I atone

We both are quite adept to fix feelings
You paint, I write poems; both of love healings

Bumpy In Stride

I just sailed in, didn't give her a chance
That's my usual way, scant warning given
But I will charm her with winsome boy's dance
She'll then recall fondly passions driven

I did explain not to take me grievous
Nor that I be overly amorous then said
For my poems are written of those parlous
To help them get over sadness when had

I have figured it out; loves angst, mad as
Can be; has to be the feeling that rocks
That does not take sides of social status
But screws with all our lives, evens the knocks

So tell me now, are you willing to ride
As the journey can be bumpy in stride

But Then Came a Boston Juliet

It rained hard and washed the tiles of debris
Sparrows are out of luck, spilled food is gone
They'll beg for scraps, what you'll give them for free
Scrounging like most here, work almost is none

It's much cooler so I wonder about
Will it stay this way or back to summer
Days of dry heat that tax coolers output
And make sleeping a chore, more a bummer

I felt good this morning, is that then why
This poem's rubbish, perhaps for I languor
Hardly a mood for good sonnets to ply
As those rhyming words seem only to bore

But then came a Boston Juliet, girl led
Except his name was as Caesar's misread

But You Have Guessed Correct

How you measure one's life depends what's seen
Rule one requires that the starting point known
And since most leave high school at age eighteen
That will be the jump off, the place we're sown

Rule two sets the factors used for limits
Might be retire age of sixty–five years
An age set in dogma if not permits
If set beyond then there might be arrears

Rule three is the touchstone of what's measured
For in death no further records exist
And there can't be changes made by insured
The last yard stick therefore be of theist

You may question who makes final the nod
But you have guessed correct for it is God

CAN DRAW FORTH A POEM

There is this quest unknownst yet I search on
For it draws me closer to my loved one
To rest within her arms; there now I've gone
I am secure, I have no need to run

Is this riddle about the dead Leopard
It too had a quest, so the tale is told
And the answer was found to be inward
That it had chased the wrong scent; it was cold

I too have been hunting, sniffing for scent
And found it was fresh, not at all dormant
Then in ardor I knew what this had meant
That my true love was found at that moment

Watching an old movie, especially at night
Can draw forth a poem most complex insight

CAN'T SAY WHEN

Like a soldier from war I come to you
See my scars of life's toils I show proudly
Render your hearth that I may lay down too
To sleep quiet with no past cries loudly

Only you know my grief's that I've carried
Yet you ask no questions of my travails
When I rest my head you soothe what's parried
And soon I rest complete, you've salved my ails

Is it fair I ask you that I come thus
What do I give to you besides trouble
I've few coins yet refused as too much fuss
But I leave them hidden though you grumble

Next year I'll stay, but I've said that before
Then one day (can't say when) I'll come no more

CERTAIN THEIR PLOYS

Just a picnic in the park; so simple
I then wondered why twas not thought before
Some iced cold shrimp, cheddar cheese to sample
With fruit and some veggies, such the allure

A spread blanket; we'd sit on the green grass
While I set out our lunch, a feast began
We would talk of mundane events, none crass
But short vignettes of movies we then ran

It was a most perfect time, this fall day
With warm sun and a slight breeze then blowing
From the lake the air was tanged from mowed hay
And wild flowers that framed our view showing

Oh I had help, poets are not gourmets
But when given the food certain their ploys

CLAP WITH GLEE

Mellow I feel; Michael Bublé singing
Getting me in the mood ready to write
What shall it be, sonnet or verse bringing
I'll check meter and rhyme forming; sounds right

Sunday night when she called at eight o'clock
Telling me of her trip and how it went
Asking about my book, its price shylock
Not at all as under twenty bucks spent

Now I'm lying in bed, Twinkie's grooming
Fed of Tuna she plops beside me here
She won't bother me when Bublé's crooning
We're a pair, me writing sonnets with her

I see my form; Shakespeare would clap with glee
Or would he say, there's not enough melee

Clouds Now Rolling on By

I see fluffy white clouds outside floating
Do they remind me of different objects
Squinting my eyes is that a man boating
No, that too is changing, no longer projects

I can recall when young, seeing a face
More a profile but still it was distinct
And while watching it the nose grew fast pace
Getting longer, then it bends down and kinked

Then when I was flying my view shifted
I was looking down at the clouds shadows
Were there eyes that watched these same clouds gifted
Those that lay down upon grassy meadows

As I watch these clouds now rolling on by
I ask myself did God make them and why

COME BACK IN THE SPRINGTIME

Come sit with me, listen to my night sounds
Hush now for you must be quiet to hear
There – hear that wail as the Loon intones
Catch the thump of the drum; Bullfrogs are near

The wind through the Pine trees; bowing of strings
And rat–a–tat–tatting of Wood Peckers
Beats my baton as now changes here brings
For the howls of Grey Wolves they be hecklers

Oh it is a mess now, the Swan's trumpet
When the Bees are humming; no, no I cry
You must not then bugle, that's Moose's dammit
And why are the fish bubbling their fry

Maybe you should forget, take a rain check
Come back in the springtime, this groups a wreck

Cool Now My Walk with Breeze

I took a walk; quiet this was Sunday
Garage doors were open; that was normal
A time to clean things out before Monday
When work and school duties were more formal

Passing the golf course I saw the purist
Playing around gaggles of those wild geese
That comes from our neighbor up north to rest
Goose poop on the lawns of parks, ne'er it cease

Reached now Western and the turn back corner
I had not found any golf balls on lawns
Bruce finds them for Parker, he's his garner
As a kid I'd get ten cents each at pawns

My turn complete I walk under tall trees
The sun shaded, cool now my walk with breeze

COOLER AIR WAITS INDOOR

Gently flows the Cannon when not in flood
For then its force is felt sweeping the park
Of all small twigs, branches; even firewood
But now it is serene, hardly of mark

And the day is hot; some would say onerous
A day that corn grows tall and kids will swim
Twas heat like this that felled poor Icarus
Such too, heatstroke; many will fall victim

But now I rest; do I detect a breeze
If so it would never float a feather
Still the ample trees do in time appease
And in late fall there'll be change in weather

I see the Geese have now waddled ashore
Time to pack up; cooler air waits indoor

CRYPTIC WRITINGS

I care not if they chide me for loving
For they know not my thoughts held thus closely
Let them deride me here; insults throwing
I'll not turn my back as they're fools mostly

I can hold this nugget, this small item
Here in my heart secure; just let them try
To force secrets from me for I'll fight them
And then when I'm alone dream of this nigh

If death should take me while prisons my keep
I have yet your memory, all else then gone
Let me scratch on my cell walls words most deep
Place your love here hidden, open to none

And in this cell inscribed, intoned our guide
Are some cryptic writings of one who died

Dark Chocolate Toffee

I am a most positive man; be assured
Wouldst I pursue this Norsk princess if not
Silly then your question; I'm not detoured
Only now more convinced I'll have her got

Blame it on my Navy jet flight training
There just isn't any room for error
You do it right the first time; no feigning
Wasted effort to then repeat; see there

And wouldst thou then desire a man lesser
I think not; a wimpy man is blandly
Not your cup of tea this flaccid mister
No you want me as I am now; manly

After all a man who drinks dark coffee
Might just want to taste dark chocolate toffee

Did I Scare You

Did I scare you daddy, will you now run
I'm the monster from the deepest ocean
Come now to eat all the ice cream; leave none
For you or your friends so use caution

I am here to protect Dora, my Queen
See her picture on my swimsuit tummy
I'm not really all bad, sans doute, not mean
If you do not believe me ask mommy

And these goggles, they will protect my eyes
From the fishes and small sea nymphs that swim
In the water trying to be good spies
But I know them so their antics are dim

Do you want to join me in my pool here
We'll play and splash, come on then, show no fear

Do I See a Smile Now

A pure sonnet of love I pen to you
Let then your mind wander, relish in thought
Breathe in passions bouquet, taste of me too
For all of these my poem to you now brought

Close your eyes...now picture those most wanton
Sate of daydreams; taking your fill complete
Ride the magic carpet, pretend then on
A black stallion riding until deplete

Resting now your pulse slows, then toward slumber
Whispers in your ears tell of love waiting
Then you feel lips kissing more in number
Than you can count, dare this lead to mating

Spent now you drift into a deep sleep state
Do I see a smile now that I'll relate

Do You Sense My Longing

Do you sense my longing, feel my heart beats
There that lay of walking, cat like the steps
Across your bed, but you have no such feet's
Perhaps just a fold of bedding mishaps

The thought is lost as deep slumber abides
And then a loud crack, was that too heard
Or just your mind hearing the sound insides
So now you must wonder, but that's absurd

Your mind is now searching for clues bidden
Yes, there was that sound you recall it now
Drying of floor joists or something hidden
So why do you think of him, you don't know

When fast asleep and dreams come by freely
Every touch and sound you sense comes from me

Do You Sense That Feeling

Do you love me, I mean deep down do you
With all my heart and soul I do promise
Then what do you propose; tell me no rue
As time grows short and you're not in harness

Only to love from afar, I ask no more
Simply sending fond hand written letters
Which tell of my gladness; not of dour
That we are now apart, not in fetters

From time to time I'll pen sonnets of love
To send them by parcel, first class airmail
If not by jet airplane, then by a Dove
Who will carry them more swiftly; won't fail

God how I do love you cosset of mine
Do you sense that feeling written in rhyme

Don't a Look-back Glance

Oh such beauty my eye there doth behold
I wouldst but swoon for ne'er her face to be
Then let me bask in such glory all told
For tis her that I so adore and see

Fortune lent me my friend wherewith to court
Should I ask of marriage, such would be bliss
Or should I wait; goodness, I'm not the sort
To tell secrets; of that I'd be remiss

Don't be foolish; for one deepest in love
Such coup de foudre is most common to come
Do not discard these fond feeling thereof
Rather rejoice here with complete aplomb

Seldom does one get a second romance
But if you do, then don't a look-back glance

Don't Ask Me to Dance

It's a lazy Sunday we so enjoy
Sitting around drinking our dark coffee
I to my poems; perhaps a few I'll try
Letting my mind relax; thoughts to run free

Oh I marvel at what comes forth with ease
'twere a sonnet in form that I would choose
Let then the rhyme and slow meter flow please
To end with a couplet that might amuse

Shall I write then anon; this gift I have
There seems no harm; blank verse wouldn't have come
But a pouring outflow; soothing like salve
That brings the whole picture to life as one

I'll write poems a plenty given a chance
Just let me be, please don't ask me to dance

DON'T SEND ALARM

Do you think my poems will one day be great
I mean will they honor my name famous
To be read by school girls hungered for treat
And by school boys seeking the more amorous

Or will my books gather dust in library
To be found in archives hound by students
Giving those who'd research poets the key
That will open their thoughts, give them tendance

I would rather eschew instant fame won
Simply lauded by my friends that wish to yearn
Master of rhyme and verse meter, the one
Who gives more of himself than in return

Accept me as I am, I mean no harm
But if you be concerned, don't send alarm

Eager for the Night

Comes now silent to dwell within my heart
For I welcome love the truest of friend
No great fanfare, ne'er a bugle to start
Just love quiet the way it ought to tend

It is you the sender, I know your touch
And what pleasures do you bring this night
To sate my heart, those that I love so much
Then let them now enter, they have the right

I feel it now, pleasant numbing begins
Then spreads to fill each limb and then torso
Sensate of your love my heart now beckons
Come fill every part of needs and more so

I've now slept the night in wondrous rapture
Eager for night when once more you capture

ENDLESS THE PAGES

I'm not perfect but I do some things well
Like I'll write poems each day, ne'er I forget
And make cell phone calls each night just to tell
I love you, and emailed pictures sent yet

You know my minds always working ahead
Starting a phrase, looking for rhymes that end
A line or a couplet; what then was said
So each poem is fresh with meaning portend

I do love to travel; Norway sounds great
But just a road trip that explores your State
Would be grand too for I could write poems late
At night with you snuggled beside me mate

I do perpend that I'll perdure ages
To write sonnets of love, endless the pages

ERICA

Her red hair cascading while she shovels
A more kindled woman I can't imagine
She could drive a stagecoach, skip in gambols
Ice fish in the cold, yet remains fem'nine

She greets me with a smile; hello Poet
Serves me quickly; coffee and day–old scone;
Want that warmed: no need to ask, she knows it
As I retreat to my table alone

Mother too, a baby boy named Stephen
Twenty months old, a real bundle of joy;
Works the machines making lattes; even
Cleans the tables, yet to men she acts coy

Erica reminds me of Ruben's model
A warm hearted woman, full to cuddle

Essence of What You Said

To write a love sonnet is quite easy
But you must then recall of the rhyming
As this line rhymes easy; could be mazy
So don't get lost, it might spoil your timing

Now that the scheme is known, you'll just repeat
This for two more stanzas; so on to love
If he is most special, then you'll entreat
Him to return same; that which we spoke of

Tell him that he's always there in your heart
Let him know that parting, even for days
Wears most heavy; that there seems a rampart
Has been built to keep him from overstays

In this couplet; essence of what you said
A two–liner, rhymed, with hinting instead

EVER FAITHFUL CAT

Hey there Twinkie, jump up here on my bed
For you've been fed Tuna fish, red and lean
I know I said no more after last fed
For you left some droppings for me to clean

But I'm such a softy; just a small cry
From you and there melts my anger away
And this just lets you know that just one sigh
Will cause me to forget past scat left stray

There must be a reason that I do this
It could be your sex as I'm just putty
To fold and mold by the woman I miss
But that's silly, you'd find me then nutty

Once more I write of her linkage to my
Ever faithful cat that near me doth lie

EVER I LOOK BACK

There will be a few that take this to heart
That I only wished to write of love gone
And how mistakes may have ripped me apart
That it's easy to look back once upon

What I have are memories of life before
Please grant my mind not to fail of recall
As my poems would cease thus freezing the score
And I have more, oh yes, much to enthrall

But I have lived through these many mistakes
Perhaps they weren't as bad as I made out
For don't we all stumble along with aches
A fact of life; doesn't love pain throughout

Ever I look back, such joy it brings me
For my futures not that distant I see

EVERY PERSON FORECASTS THE SKY

Lightning flashes; does that mean rain tonight
Are you talking to me kid; said Sir Weather
It was just a puzzle; mystery of sight
That made me ask; Sir, no offense either

Forget it kid, I get the brunt of jokes
You do know I don't have special insights
What is coming is that; coming now folks
And I can't turn it off; I have no rights

But you do warn people when there are storms
Yes; but that is okay; plaudits when right
And when wrong; then people forget informs
No son, the worst case is sunny at night

I keep quiet I'm Sir Weather; know why
It is because every person forecasts the sky

Fed My Muse Which I Own

You know it is pretty easy to write
A line jotted down, then inklings of verse
Seem to appear like pure magic in sight
Should I give thanks; then to whom I say terse

These thoughts may be floating around my head
Waiting to be captured; then put to use
But how many escape, never get read
Are they stuck in cobwebs hidden from muse

You speak I have talent, should I agree
Get puffed of my moment, aloof they'd say
That might not be correct; fustian maybe
And I suppose you could mention outré

It took over an hour to write this down
But I had lunch, fed my muse which I own

First Love to Cherish

We sit apart except for brief moments
When we talk and when I visit Faribault
Our lives detached yet great ease still ferments
That bonds our souls affined by love thorough

You were my first of love, full of wonder
When a kiss sent rapture to my hearts core
And your smile would only make me fonder
When I would greet you in school halls of yore

And why shouldn't we still embrace fondness
Our hearts were once combined in love buoyant
Cheerful and suave we were in youth's caress
Little we knew of the import love meant

These my memories of first love to cherish
Let them spur our friendship not to perish

First on Love

Must we speak of mundane money matters
Where is romance mentioned when bills are paid
How can a check writ match with love letters
Or bank deposit compare with iced–tea made

That we both have lived our lives in comfort
Does that not tell that when combined no ill
Shall then befall as we then can support
Cheaper as two than each singly of bill

You must excuse if I believe strongly
That the man still provides comforts of home
But if matched then surely this not wrongly
Offered as our unions written in poem

We build marriage first on love and then trust
Always to be truthful, caring and just

FOR GOD'S ALWAYS THERE

When you recite your prayers you talk with God
That's a big deal when you're young and wounded
When you feel all adults simply are odd
And grand mother is far away grounded

You must always feel God is at your call
Any time and any place you can meet
For it doesn't need be bedtime at all
You can talk at breakfast or on your feet

And God has a memory; he won't forget
What you have prayed for, but don't you expect
Instant relief; no, it must fit so let
His grand scheme play out, the perfect collect

Now when you pray let God be your best friend
For God's always there or around the bend

For I Am the Rainbows End

Are you awake my love; cooed forth the Dove
For he brings you such gladness of my love
Ah, he sees you stirring; his deed is done
And flies away; you cry...leave me then none

I'm here purrs the kitten; hold me gently
And I'll lick your face, then nibble of thee
But this tires too quickly; this was no fun
Tiki's after me; I better then run

Have you been teased enough my Norsk Princess
They have done their jobs well I must confess
But it takes a man like me to wake you
To plant that first kiss; a start, oh so true

Have my minions served me; truly they have
For I am the rainbow's end and your fave

For I'm New to This

It's a lovely thought even if unnamed
When I think of being with you next year
Can I control ardor that runs untamed
I can when I let my poems speak clear

Tis then romance I pen with my sonnets
Letting you read amour; is this my part
Making my spell surround you by comets
Their tails showering angel's dust on your heart

Then off again my mind wanders aimless
In a daze I see the flowers blooming
But tis winter I cry; oh what a mess
For there is my love now in the gloaming

Is it then a sickness that makes me numb
For I am new to this; crazy become

FOR THE CIRCLES COMPLETE

I felt it as soon as I had entered
Perhaps kindred was the feeling inside
As it whelmed my heart; join with us tendered
And of course I agreed; brimming with pride

Suppose, I thought; how quaint it must appear
Whisker–like corn stubble; for my own face
It too showed the wear of my trip to here
Roughly hewn the resolve; ne'er then erase

I watched as my body; skipping along
Each time picking up some chunks of top soil
Until I was one and the same of song
Truly now borne; my Norse spirit would toil

Welcome home now traveler; you've earned the right
For the circles complete; wholeness in sight

For They Can't See of Love

Of your hair so faire in color auburn
That brushes my face as I embrace and hold
To kiss, ah the rapture I take in turn
Tis your auburn in sun now made of gold

Wouldst these moments lasting, alas they end
As at your gate closing my love departs
Show your face from window my love my friend
And I shall then linger, entwined our hearts

On my way home I feel not the rainfall
Or mud puddles that soak my step into
Perceive his face beaming, whence comes withal
And he's singing, what has this world come to

But I just smile for they can't see of love
Not like mine, a boy of twelve that knows of

FOR THIS I SHALL SUFFER

Is this folly that I wish of your love
Tell me; no...from your lips I plead silence
Let me bask in daydreams; yet you reprove,
I can sense so clearly; clewing riddance

Let me offer my love as a locket
That you can wear around your neck on chain
Then from time to time, when saddened, touch it
And like genies lamp, I'll comfort your pain

I shant require that you return in same
That would be too much to ask for I know
Yet still there's that ember to keep aflame
And it only requires a kiss to glow

Still, I writhe in anguish of my making
For this I shall suffer in my waking

FOR TO DIE FROM LOVE

What could be a better way to show love
Than to write a sonnet just for you here
Putting these words down on paper tell of
What's been within my heart, afraid to bare

Only too then embrace, feel your heart beats
Meld them with my shattered heart now pestled
Then to press my hungered lips for your treats
Of tastes sublime and there remain nestled

If I could hold you for ever I would
And to smell your essence, such sweet perfumed
Drunken with love, oh such joy that I should
Let my stone read; he died of love consumed

Then my life is fulfilled and my poem lore
For to die from love one can ask no more

For You This is Written

For you this is written, heed what I say
That for every waking moment my thoughts
Are for only of you; thus hear my lay
To clutch near your bosom all of my broughts

I bring laughter where it's needed to heal
And a smile most warming brightening your day
I will teach you phrases that you can feel
That sends your heart thumping blithely you'll say

And when winter snows all carpet your lawn
I'll trace angels, my arms flailing all free
And build rotund snowman with red–nosed fawn
These things I'll bring you as you dream of me

You are my love, my soft cosset to hold
And though I am afar these words are told

Found Gold

I know you love me, I can feel it now
For it hastens my step as I journey
Did I mention my trip, where I would go
No, I suspect not; but it's Killarney

Two months ago you were sleeping; an Elf appeared
I was afraid you'd be wakened; she shook her head
I knew then the message was what I feared
You must visit dear old Ireland; she said

By the time you have read this I've arrived
The Black Valley of the Gap of Dunloe
Is my intent and not something connived
She said; search for the gold by the rainbow

Darling, wake up; you were mumbling; "foretold"
And I believe you did mention; "found gold"

FROM GREEN TO YELLOW THENCE GOLD

I'm at peace with myself here in St. Croix
Where the river tumbles, least to the dam
To call it a falls, well tempers your joy
But the tree leaves in fall, gorgeous here, damn

There was a flour mill here; Thompson grains well
Were they from old Norway, the name rings true
Before that logs were sent floating pell–mell
But that went bust when the dam's specs went through

It's so tranquil, almost serene in fall
A cool wind blows from the north, does it bode
Winter to come soon; stay away I call
Let these days now linger, autumns my mode

I'll write again on the morrow of trees
That from green to yellow thence gold is these

Fuel For One Tasked

It so happened that two were sent to Mars
Why two you asked; simple as the capsule
Could seat only pair; no single takers
Of course as one backup was needed, the rule

Fate would have it, one of God, the other
Converse of all belief; inverse of his pair
The first tiff came on launch; does prayer bother
Well I'm sorry, that's not allowed as fair

Then in orbit around Mars, by hand did
Descend; a smooth touchdown was made as planned
The first out said; by God's grace we've landed
His pair remarked; by my hand was manned

That eve aboard the Mars Lander, God asked
Which of you will remain; fuel for one tasked

Full of Zest

I lay there a moment, my thoughts at ease
And soon recall your face, oh most pleasant
Then in esteem to write; my pen I seize
With such sweetness flows, my line thus descant

Shall I tell a secret; poems come freely
When I think of you here; as in rapture
My hand pens love ballads most smooth really
I should have to pay for what I capture

Now I can rise again and then perdure
My trek across this land; wondrous this day
As I search for knowledge; gainsay impure
Thoughts and deeds for poets too need to pray

But I have now given you of my best
Thus my sonnets tell of love full of zest

Girls That Admire

Do you recall the soapbox derby races
When your brother scrounged all about the house
Looking for wheels, ropes and orange boxes
Then to the car garage; more there to browse

Then he'd laid all his loot out on the floor
And closed the door; this was secret to all;
For days after school he'd all but ignore
His friends; then rush inside, grab a meatball

On the Fourth of July, wrapped in bunting
He'd rolled his prize outdoors with much acclaim
Then to the hill where the others all were daunting
The green flag then lowered; he rode to fame

Gathered in a circle, girls that admire
His skill building a soap box car suspire

GRANT ME THE WISDOM

I looked into the water; twas quite still
And saw the face so long now forgotten
Then it mouthed a message; love is tranquil
When you're pursued in faith not ill–gotten

Then the wind sprang up and rippled my view
That night I thought hard upon what I'd learned
Did the message mean stable; calm knew
In my heart; that your love was not wicked

That this steady, relentless love was what
I had desired; that we were of like minds
Thus these thoughts were balm to my heart; a shot
Of freshness that had awakened reminds

I prayed then to God; grant me the wisdom
That my love be tender, joyful, fulsome

HAD HE BEEN HERE

I peeked in last night when you were asleep
And stood just inside the door; quietly
Tiptoed to your side; Tiki, not a peep
And looked in wonder; no sounds; silently

I covered you where the blanket had fell
Leaving one arm exposed; you didn't wake
Then I sat on the couch for just a spell
Listening to the night sounds till dawn would break

I then arose and softly kissed your lips
A slight stir but then you relaxed again
Tiki saw me; from the glass he took sips
Then settled down, his day not yet began

When I was gone; nothing left to appear
You'd wonder this morning, had he been here

HAD OUR LIFE BEEN DIFFERENT

Lass your beauty never faded away
Twas I that saw through eyes muddled by fate
Of bent image that was myself of clay
And not of you, wonder of all things great

I have been touched; were you asked then about
Or has my lame conscience done this alone
Of that much doubt, indeed it came from out
A gift wondrous that I peruse till known

Let me write of life, to show its ribbing
It's past glories, of love stable and errs
May my subject be then ever jibing
That may excite the mind of my readers

Oh lass you know withal this comes from me
Had our life been different would this poem be

HARD WORK LIKE OUR FOREBEARS

There's a sense of calmness that now appears
For it pervades throughout every household
Some say that from the South; others, one hears
Express their doubt amid fears now grown bold

Is it because of that damned name it came
To be ravaged by hell; will of the gods
To some eyes a monster; one they can't tame
That eats up the land and swallows in gobs

One can suppose that in time it will end
A place torn and battered unfit to see
Can we say with credence misery will mend
That once more the spirit festive to be

I'll give you the answer; spare me your tears
Hard work like our forebears placates those fears

He Wants Actors That Try

Go thou nicely and smell the sweet nectar
Then breathe deeply and let loose of trouble
Tis of joy then, so go forth young actor
For on this day you'll play another's double

For our Bard, the William Shakespeare, directs
And he has asked specially that you appear
To play Hamlet, a role without defects
But be forewarned, the Bard's choice still unclear

Then tell me, how goes the play called Hamlet
I've heard the part demands some sword fighting
I have thought of that, you'll wear a gauntlet
But make no doubts, Hamlet's his best writing

This is your big chance; look him in the eye
Speak most loudly, he wants actors that try

Hearing Echoes by Choice

Lovely her voice; was that I just heard now
Echoes that were bounced off the walls of rock
Like the bells then pealing near the Moldau
Could not compare to what I would unlock

There was ringing in my eardrums daily
Try as I may I could not stop this sound
It was touching my work at Old Bailey
What could I do, her voice held me spellbound

Late at night I would walk along the Thames
It was quiet and the noise was reduced
Perhaps I would met her; like my poems
I'd ask; why in god's name was I ill–used

I've told Doctor Faustus about her voice
He has said; I'm hearing echoes by choice

HEART SHAPED WROTE SHE

I love waking with you in the morning
Little stretches and you're shifting around
It's then that I want you; such love yearning
As I guide you to my chest; your warmth found

Its pure pleasure; your head resting anon
Then the softness of your body; points touch
And I feel the current surge; then it's gone
You have smothered my whole; ne'er there an ouch

Your eyes look deep within my soul; then wait
For me to clasp; pressing you most tender
To fit my length, my leg between; a fait
As you settle gently; your thoughts too render

I can tell that this is going to be
A most wondrous morning; heart shaped wrote she

HE'S DONE HIS JOB

Pumpkins, largest of farm grown, gourd–like squash
You see them piled on flats ready to sell
As you travel farm roads, asking for cash
They're three or four dollars the signs will tell

And they're not all orange, some are yellow
And of sizes to charm children to pick
The ones they want outside saying, hello
From their carved mouths, do you want treats or trick

In late fall when temps, like in your freezer
And ice forms on the lakes, features transform
On the pumpkin's face; he looks the geezer
With his mouth slumped down, gums toothless the norm

Then mom will say; let's put pumpkin away
He's done his job, his seeds we'll plant today

Hoping For a Reply

Oh Will, do I work the fool now in turn
For it is hard playing at love these years
I wouldst wish a hint now and then to earn
Fair my maidens kiss thus taken midst fears

For I have a problem, my loves now gone
Straight to Paris where a follies she'll be
She says a class act but I shant condone
Until I hear from you, knowing what be

I fear I shall never be a poet
That ranks as you; forgive my poor lament
But it wears hard on one whose love go'ith
Should I write prose or pen plays most fervent

I will send this letter quickly to thee
Hoping for a reply that will help me

Hoping That Once Again

I thought about what I had said before
When I was in a funk; heavens knows why
Cramming so much into our lives; encore
I felt I was drowning, thus then my cry

For years I have thought that perhaps someday
We would meet; oh the dreams were of delight
And then it did happen and was, I say
Special and yet over in just a night

Now I have had time to ponder, to think
And I like the steady progress we make
No flash in the pan, no romance on brink
We grow closer, then let distances forsake

I shall of course have dreams about you here
Hoping that once again we'll meet a pair

How the Leaves Lay Stilled

The bow was drawn, then the signal given
And the arrow flew true, it was made well
Sunlight seen to glint as breastplate riven
Declan near, was thunder struck; his Sire fell

Ronan foaming was now pawing the ground
His red drape hung loosely, now blocked the sun
But the word would soon spread by mouth around
Then Sire beckoned Declan; saddle Rogan

Sire in show of strength took off his helmet
Put this on and ride the lines, they'll think I
For you can win now this battle as met
Then leave me here with Shaun for I will die

In the ensued years the story was told
How the leaves lay stilled as no wind enfold

I Am At Peace

I am at peace; music of Grieg playing
And all I can think of is life with you
I won't make it abstruse for I'm saying
It quite plainly my loves honest and true

I am at peace; listening, hearing birds sing
Their trills express my joy, they have sensed it
And come to join with me; banter they bring
And I shall then enjoy laughter and wit

I am at peace; come soon we'll be conjoined
For I love you dearly; my heart cries out
Come take me now as to you I'm consigned
Let it be known to all what loves about

I can hardly hold back ardor's feeling
When I know that soon you'll give me healing

I Am the Sly Sandman

Doth thou see me when you dream and night falls
And my image remains in clear focus
I would hope that occurs, that it enthralls
Your heart with hope; not of hocus–pocus

I have so much to give to you of love
Rapture when you are near dreaming, asleep
Thoughts of rolling hills in flower behove
Blissful now as slumbered thoughts of me seep

These are moments when I will plant the seed
That in time grows; blossoms in gay splendor
Then when awake the thoughts clear; there the deed
Is right before you and you must render

I am the sly sandman that dabs your eyes
With the magic powder that causes sighs

I AM YOUR SIGHT TO BEHOLD

Love is a time of much wonder and fret
Because it is complex and holds with sway
And this feeling outranks even beget
Has God then meant that it would be this way

I too feel love special and I'm willing
To take the downs with the ups of romance
Nothing is then sweeter than a thrilling
Kiss and embrace after a spat of chance

You need me to assist in chores right here
And be assured it's not duty, but love
As I want to spend my life with you dear
And pray that God will see me fit, above

Sweet the wonder is here; the frets away
For I am your sight to behold soigné

I Can Relate to That

There is a dog barking, that much I know
It could be a squirrel has piqued his wrath
Or that he (she) wants some notice although
Now I hear no more so perhaps a gaff

Today the group goes to Jeanie and Dick's
About a half–hour drive, should be pleasant
Carroll, Max and Bruce my erstwhile sidekicks
Will make chatter, as I drive, with descant

Our goal is Clear Lake, south of west of here
A new condo we look forward seeing
That is if their puppy hasn't cause wear
And tear of their sofas and floor peeing

I can relate to that as my cat's scat
Is placed, when she's upset, where I have sat

I Guess That Would Depend

Those tones affect me, I can feel serene
Why they do I have no answer either
Are there workings afoot to fool my scene
To make me feel sad and lonely further

Maybe in my doldrums I feel of late
There at night when only I hear music
Forlorn in thought; laments of my heartache
I will reflect on what I think most basic

And that would be concepts for poems written
Which puts me back to how music impels
And am I now in a closed loop smitten
Almost like a merry–go–round compels

And what were those accents of tone therein
I guess that would depend what mood I'm in

I Have Always Returned

You knew it would happen; that I'd call you
As I had thought, perhaps this is the time
Guessing you might be in Devils Lake too
I dialed and held my breath; your voice, sublime

And in a mere instant the world flowered
And bells and shouts were heard; I'd swear
It was as if the Earth had just showered
And all objects around fresh en plein air

I know you have feelings that are elsewhere
That your family takes your thoughts now away
But my love grows stronger; like a fanfare
It blares to my heart; have patience and stay

Even the times that I've cloistered my love
I have always returned; this I've pledged of

I Have Solved Greater of Doubts

These past months have been as her consort
So my leaving becomes our first parting
And though I do expect it shall be short
The time away will draw heavy the sting

To ease our pain we shall call most frequent
And send emails to and fro with our love
We did all this before and fine it went
As then later we can savor thereof

I shall write my poems and send them forthwith
Spending my eves writing in bed of her
And she can paint; perhaps of scenes wondro'th
That can bring us closer then, much sooner

I look forward; blotting out those abouts
After all I have solved greater of doubts

I Hear You Snoring

He's a big Blue Standard Poodle named Mo
And a service dog to boot, so he says
I see the red jacket you wear says so
Do you wear it always or just Wednesdays

You do see the little white dog looking
Her names Frieda and is a Jack Russell
A young gal too, age four; want a booking
I might have an agent that will hustle

There goes Nikki riding on the scooter
Which means you are alone with the Sparrows
Don't waste your time, they could use a tutor
They're not able to speak or shoot arrows

Now you have laid down, am I that boring
I say again...oh, I hear you snoring

I Hope You'll Not Mind of Slander

Strange beasts, they come in chains setting on laps
Not more than ten pounds of weight I would guess
Bred of fierce bent, threatened myself with yaps
They shout beware of my bite, you trespass

Some come with the mark of purist of breed
But are often coupled with a bastard
As if to show; see there, lesser has peed
By the table, your legged jambeau on guard

Their names were like Benji, some called Baby
Have their owners naught of genius to call
For I could give Canis major for free
And the Canis minor, half–breed you–all

Goodbyes were said; yes I do write sonnets
I hope you'll not mind of slander; your pets

I Knew She Was Irish

I knew she was Irish, red hair foretold
I said to her; you are Irish aren't you
Glancing towards me; yes, she said quite bold
Then the concert started, my thoughts ran new

During a short music respite I said
I too am of Irish blood, well maybe
But then music began and talk fell dead
While the singers belted out melody

When the concert finished, I said please wait
I have for you my book; sonnets they are
Perhaps I may write you, ask of their fate
If you're pleased I'll pen one for you with care

As we passed near at night much came to know
This glance that showed more than a brief hello

I Pledge Now Here

What can I say, only that we be friends
It is special, there are no fast rules spoke
Unlike a love affair it has no ends
But goes through thick and thin even when broke

I've thought long and hard, this must be the way
For you both know I will return to home
And may never return again to stay
As each year we age, travel hard to come

I will perdure as a poet, thus said
You may receive love poems written by me
Because being a friend, fervent I'm led
It is my sole nature; loving I be

So let us stay our course, remain as were
The charmed circle ever I pledge now here

I Saw You Fly Away

Don't fly away; I beg of you please stay
I'll not harm you, I just want to wonder
What it is like flying; is it like play
Letting the wind carry you there yonder

Such bright eyes you have are you now searching
Looking for a meal of Lizard or plumb field Mouse
Or just resting in those branches parching
As the Sun's hot, but then you're soon to rouse

I've seen you drink water, little beak sips
Then fluff feathers, but you soon flew to perch
On that power pole there making head dips
Is that because you are always on search

I saw you fly away, your minds made–up
To the river, find a dead fish to sup

I Send My Son

Thor, Norse god of thunder, weather and crops
Well, I have a weather person degree
And you might say thunder came when dewdrops
Formed then amid lightning which hit a tree

But what of crops for I have scant interest
Then this is your intro, spreading the seed
A Norse goddess of course, willing, earnest
She will implant our stock, devils too need

I shall call you Inga; prairie flower
So sweet amid grass thick, rich in protein
Where a seed then planted grows much slower
But such a rich harvest ne'er was then seen

But I have not finished, I send my son
Thence to appear whence doubt became to one

I Shall

Shall I tell you dear how much I love you
For it grows each moment that we're apart
Shall I tell you of my longing to woo
To bring you close to me, our life to start

Shall I shout it from the roof tops loudly
So all the world may hear the joy within
Shall I shout I love you standing proudly
My friends gathered round me, assured I'll win

Shall I pledge with ardor my life entwined
To be beside you whenever the need
Shall I pledge to protect from thoughts opined
That wants to take you from me to succeed

I shall tell and shout and pledge my love here
That I'm in your soul your heart your self dear

I SHALL READ MY POEMS TO YOU

Love doth caress with the sunrise this morn
And is renewed again when the moon's full
So it is on these days that my loves born
To grow in time as you ponder and mull

I will take care of you; assist each day
With those things that a man's happy to do
I will love your grand kids and watch them play
And tell bedtime stories with you there too

Then we can spend winters in the southwest
With plane trips back and forth staying in touch
With the family doing the things knownst best
We shall be then teammates that I will vouch

I shall read my poems to you each morning
Cheering your heart, brightening as you're journeying

I Shall Return Of Course

Hold me tightly she cried; hold me tis right
Her frail body shaking; what could I do
Thus to enfold her in my arms; ne'er fight
But lie in pure rapture the whole night through

Oh Lord Duke must you run; leave me to fume
For I'm lonely and the winter's air blows
Cold now upon the door to my bedroom
And you know how to warm the draft on hose

But dear Manon you've kept me here two weeks
And my friend Smythe wonders what ill befalls
His tired master; I fear that he now seeks
And is in great distress and may make calls

I shall return of course; how could I not
As the spring thaw is months away I'm taught

I Shall Shed My Tear

Let me hold you once more, that's all I ask
Then let me look into your eyes there deep
Will I see what mine saw; lovers that bask
In sheer pleasure of each other complete

Then please tell me that you too feel this way
That our hearts beat as one, our breaths in sync
And I will take you to delights that lay
Beyond what mere mortals ever could think

I will woo you, enclose you in my arms
So then drop your defense, accept me now
Lay swooned upon my bed, dwell not of harm
For I will be gentle, my love of thou

But should I see within your orbs of fear
Then let me leave you, I shall shed my tear

I SPEAK FEW TONGUES

My heart and all that it matters goes forth
To you now this evening alone; alas
I can only send love posthaste of course
And to you one travels; myself then as

I shall be your beacon should need arise
But that could be years to go with best care
So I'll provide loving prayers for your eyes
And we will see the world, perhaps by air

I will dazzle you with oral readings
Of my sonnets and poems; perhaps an ode
Then of books I'll flavor with my greetings
Of each braggart, pipsqueak, yahoo and toad

You will laugh at accents; I speak few tongues
Then just blame it on the size of my lungs

I Swear to All

Oh that you speak of love that once betrayed
I swear my heart that no fonder love has I
That you are my comfort, my life thus made
As God would then punish if I did lie

From the Rose sweet nectar is born in Hips
So too will my love give forth then of pleasure
Ne'er fool as caught in the plane of ellipse
That sends love round about in small measure

My heart laid out beating asks you to take
And when then clasp to breast to keep always
Then my gift of love, truth and faith I make
As the Rose blooms ever throughout our days

This is my gage d'amour, my pledge of love
I swear to all in god's Heaven this of

I TAKE NO PAY

I'm here alone, sipping my dark coffee
Skipping my bran muffin; lunch with Michael
A break in my routine, yet here I'll be
Trying to keep going my poem cycle

Sunday next is Poet's meeting at one
It will be a double event that day
For it is my birthday; seventy–six done
I'll write a poem; perform to mark my say

I would wish for only that you were here
As these get–to–gathers produce much fun
And the formats simple; one's poems most dear
A max of three or five minutes the run

I'm known by all; sonnets are my métier
As I read these for free, I take no pay

I TASTE YOUR KISS

Does one kiss last ever in time I ask
For your lips were cool to my soft touch there
And I can taste the tang; there now, I bask
For should I die no greater love doth bear

There was this short moment when life was full
And thoughts of you infused my heart throughout
No more I've cried, let peace instill each pull
Of pure rapture err it tears love about

I will dwell in gardens flowered profuse
For their scents now hide the essence of you
There I will love amid bees of no use
A place proper for me, imbued in rue

Scores of years have passed and I face abyss
Yet from bowels of death I taste your kiss

I WANT DANCING

Dance the Sergeant had said; I want dancing
We looked askance; who was this guy kidding
Here we've hiked ten miles and he wants us prancing
We're off to war; this drill master's quitting

Hold on you grunts; I said dancing begins
These last few miles you will do as I say
I mean the waltzes and not the cancans
And then foxtrots; I want you to feel gay

Hey Sarg; what is this crap you'll have us do
We're all Marines; this soft shoe is crazy
Have you ever been where a mine field blew
No Sarg; well if you do it's a mazy

I want dancing to make your step nimble
Sometimes a straight march might cause a rumble

I Will Never Forget, Ever that Kiss

I will never forget, ever that kiss
And the strange but pleasant feeling that grew
Then that silly retort (must have been bliss)
There were trumpets and drum rolls, I bet too

What I regret (not that it had happened)
But that we were so young, like new born foals
All legs and such prancing about we'd wend
Our way along, full of spirit toward goals

Oh I shant now regret then our parting
For we are blessed truly with our children
And to suggest other than is nothing
As all those years wouldn't exist nor ken

Sometimes fortunes appear out of nowhere
Like that first kiss now bound through time to here

I Will Tell You What Love Is

I will tell you what love is if you wish
It is thinking about someone each day
Praying that they are safe; finding their niche
Cheering them when they're sad; wanting to play

Praising their deeds, giving sanctions when due
Opening the door, fixing a meal of likes
Sending a Rose on their birthday in lieu
Of a card, or better, going on hikes

Telling of your day's work even when dull
It is sharing with each other that counts
Giving of your time; just living life full
Reading to a child a story, any amounts

When all's done you needn't say I love you
As it will be well known by them that knew

I'd Charge Just a Penny

I have often wondered if love is real
Does it have form, can you see it clearly
Are those that are blinded by love of zeal
Is true love then different than love ruly

Then what of loves passion that's nixed by fate
Is that also real since fates a wild card
Dealt to either without regrets abate
I say fie as love lives, not as canard

Then what of mere friendship, is then romanced
Denied, that pulse quickness that warms one's heart
I say friendship and love are both enhanced
For love without friendship is soon to part

I wish I could bottle love and sell it
I'd charge just a penny for a kit

If I Kiss You

If I hold this thought, say it twice over
And the next day repeat it like before
Would it imprint on your mind a lover
Who is shy and cannot express love more

If I write a sonnet with words tender
Of fine romance that cause racing of heart
Would it beckon you to perhaps gender
A warm feeling for this poet upstart

If I tell you of my passion held back
How it cause much turmoil within my soul
Wouldst thou assuage the pain tortured by rack
And free me whole thence to rest here withal

If I kiss you with lips tender and sweet
Would this then be pleasure that you would greet

IF NOT ENOUGH FOR YOU

I will save those things most valued for you
And I don't mean jewelry, cars or advice
No what I have in mind outshines these too
As one item is; I'm sincere and nice

Well you wouldn't want a liar or grouch
Even diamonds and pearls are bribes only
Being mean then only makes you say ouch
So I give you item two; friendship fondly

A friend will be with you through thick and thin
A staunch bulwark that will protect always
And will not be a self–serving has been
So I give you the third; love for all days

So I'm a good guy, a friend and lover
If not enough for you then pick the other

If One You Should Question

We'll sit snuggled in bed every evening
Sipping our milk, munching away cookies
Or dark chocolate; they're good, healthy eating
Or so I tell myself taking look sees

Do you like word games; George C. Scott wonders
As he visits his dear nephew's party
If you answer yes, then I too do chairs
Where one's removed each verse; sit down smartly

I used to do crosswords; maybe again
As I do have a knack with words in poems
But they're like card games; most likely a pain
No, I'd rather snuggle and hear soft moans

Darling, words can be soft; I like these best
If one you should question; likely a jest

IF THE WORDS USED

Should I not then partake of things foolish
Am I so staid that a laugh would harm me
What's your life if being proper the wish
A dull one for certain; no cup of tea

One could write like Ogden Nash I suppose
Then do light verse, jocose, perhaps witty
That might tic my brain cells out of repose
Even right now I might pen a ditty

But hold on there partner, this here's sonnet
And not the frame to which jocund thought rules
But much rather lyric and belle facet
As one might then describe precious jewels

Maybe in the form of sonnet a jest
Could be written if the words used were geste

I'll Come Back Next Morning

Do you see me peeking behind the Birch
Look real hard; there, do you see me waving
I shant scamper further, the Queen doth perch
Above in top branches while we're laving

I watch you too every moment I get
Sitting at your easel looking askance
Do you ponder colors of leaves; I bet
It just depends on the mood felt perchance

In the winter when the snow is falling
And frost opaque's your view, do you wonder
Where we have gone, for you miss my calling
I can vision you just staring yonder

Ah, now you see me for I see your wave
I'll come back next morning, you are my fave

I'll Give Them a Song

Hey look what the cat dragged in, that's a pun
Yah, the poet he doth returneth well fed
Suppose he wants coffee and Bran muffin
Taken to his table; right now he's said

Hello there my pets; miss me, I bet you did
I've been traveling, been back to my hometown
Stayed with a friend and saw classmates ibid.
Carleton and St. Olaf; poems abound

Cut the chatter poet, did you see her
She who you've been pining for all these months
Yes...Is that all; come on tell us further
No...Cripes he's clammed up, he must think us dense

My cat friends think they know me, well they're wrong
When it comes to love I'll give them a song

I'll Shoot No Arrow

Oh my Anna how does me so adore
Your voice as it rings through my heart open
To catch such of treble you sing and more
To hold ever, thus I savor bliss in

Deep down I feel it rise slowly to warm
As light shivers pulsate my body
And in transport of sheer rapture doth swarm
Within my head, I'm now feeling giddy

So I shall lie upon my bed this night
And feel comfort not felt this way before
As the music of your soul floats with height
Never ending lulling me with encore

I must worship you from afar you know
Ever our paths cross I'll shoot no arrow

I'll Take My Chance

Do you really think someone's out there
Someone who will see the merits I bring
Who will devote, full-time, as my commère
One that to all accounts of my liking

I think it is doubtful in my trav'ln
For an affair to spring-up on the road
I would need to appear as one grav'ln
Hawking myself as a ware; not my mode

I see this trip getting some poems written
Taking pictures, eating at small cafés,
Spending time at wifi hot spots gotten,
Talking with the locals; drinking coffees

Now, if you can see where I might enhance
Getting contacts, tell me; I'll take my chance

I'll Type It Up

What's that smile I see on your face Poet
No, don't tell me...so soon; you just got back
Better take your snowshoes; go on; do it
You're more blissful up north and you've got tact

I should say, no comment, like those lawyers
But that wouldn't be me in a nutshell
So the answer is yes, I am going to hers
But I'll bed down at a local motel

Listen, it is crucial that I'm earnest
And not a fly in your face jet jockey
Something has changed in my makeup and best
She knows I'm not the crass name for Donkey

So I have now penned to her a sonnet
I'll type it up and send it sans edit

In My Mind to Exist

Roberds Lake, I always said soft Roberds
But with ending 'erts'; Pat wanted it 'erds'
How could I then explain this word I'd reared
So it was best to be silence inferred

The old bathhouse is gone, no more swimming
For boats hang at dockside gently bobbing
There are pools in Faribault, water brimming
With girls and boys, fathers sit there nodding

I'll take the road north that surrounds the Lake
Perhaps a few cabins I will recall
When mom and her deaf girls, camping she'd take
I was quite young, well too young to love all

Another spot now can be crossed off my list
Memories only in my mind to exist

In Your Heart Resting

How can I tell you how much I love you
Mere words are not enough I'm well aware
There are not stars equal to the sum knew
That would reach your heart; my love to declare

We met, perhaps it was a fluke you said
But I believe divine help was there too
Sitting in my chair I felt you instead
And knew then this woman, this love was you

It's not easy to love a man older
'Specially one that measures score plus seven
In this regard then I must act bolder
For I expect not much help here given

My love is then ceaseless; it is nesting
To have and to hold in your heart resting

Irish Elves Had No Cause

Queen may we come out, the Irish have left
Hasten to my cloaking, I will take all
But the Fairies fastened appeared bereft
For this cool glen was most pleasant withal

Where will you take us Queen one brave whispered
We fly westward to the River Shannon
Thence north to Lough Ree in County Lonford
From there we'll fly northeast; Ardagh there gone

But it's just a village, where are forests
Hush for I found a marsh and there's cover
Here we can rest, make strong our home from guests
Then in time we'll return and take over

And so the clan from far England took pause
For in their hearts Irish Elves had no cause

Its Love Spoken

Tis love I've known ever since I met her
And when I asked would she meet that evening
My heart beat most rapid, for her answer
Was yes; this bolt as by stroke of lightning

There was never any doubt in my mind
She I pursued like a fighter pilot
Not as a man on a mission, but kind
And most gallant; I'd say tender a lot

Soon the wedding and my world was complete
I could not have chosen a match better
The place I picked was the Black Cat; my beat
And was there a poem would fly to get her

Seldom does one get a second Eden
But when it does happen, its love spoken

It's Not Enough I Know

This a sonnet of joy I give to you
To hold in your heart; such warmth then becomes
That will infuse your veins, I imbue
My love so that in love sweet peace succumbs

I know I shall never give what you want
I have tried hard but the gods have stifled
A small part still gets by; do I then taunt
And tease, as you expect that I fondled

When I lay next to you my limbs tingle
Such this feeling as if god had willed it
Still if I were only; if I'd gamble
And let the odds win out as a snippet

I can only do what god has left me
It's not enough I know, pleasure for thee

It's the Honest Way

Tis more simple I'll say of our courtship
Why waste our time when the bliss comes our way
Then we'll throw no more time being gossip
And tie the knot at the Black Cat; okay

My dear, it's much more fun being married
For there's promise of sex in the margin
And with love comes the need to be honeyed
With the riches one gets in the bargain

Then I promise to hold you in rapture
To make all your troubles and fears fade out
As you're safer with me as I capture
And hold fast from harm these our lives I tout

This might be old-fashioned, but who takes heed
It's the honest way to which we'll succeed

JOIE DE VIVRE

I want to now refine my views on love
For I've wandered away, left my orbit
And find that in nothing there's not much of
Tendresse nor of pathos in those love bit

I find love is freshing, dulcet and fragrant
So full of joie de vivre and most teasing
And not at all what some refer, stagnant
Tout au contraire, most find love most pleasing

From time-to-time I must affirm this stance
Because events color my poems written
And like those that preface, love needs balance
Else those that do sample love are bitten

Pray then accept for this poem most wry'ng
Je ne sais quoi, for love is most trying

JUST MY WISHING'S

I asked you once before that we travel
And you replied; I can think of nothing
That would please me greater than to snorkel
In the warm sea looking for shells that sing

Then there was the voyage to our Norway
So much there to tell of; our roots go back
And the mountains views of Fjords far outweigh
Spending time to tour the southwest horseback

But I would be happy just to visit
The vast prairies of the land you call home
To once again write of; as a poet
Then to relax and watch where Bison's roam

I am fearful that these dreams are of such
Just my wishing's, never coming to much

Just Once Sublime

Oft I've wondered as I gaze up on high
Where clouds above unveil the great blue sky
This realm made by God so special, that I
Was blessed to be chosen as one to fly

Alone at night there's no sense of motion
It feels like you're cuddled by some giant's hands
As a gentle quiver spreads like lotion
Throughout my heart as my prowess remans

I have joined with another sister Skyhawk
As our wingmen did not launch as was planned
He gives me the lead, our mission's cakewalk
Until flak lights up the sky; no giant's hand

Quickly we dive, release our bombs on time
Wanting to be cuddled just once sublime

Keep Me Busy Thru the Winter

It was mentioned; suppose just then for worth
That dad buys a trailer, a RV type
So he could then travel this spring up north
And spend time with friends, no bother the hype

I like this and dislike it too because
The con: never before have I done this
The pro: not a burden on friends, in–laws
And I could then follow my heart of bliss

Knowing my thoughts, perchance think it over
I need input; is this a wild pitch thrown
That will lose the ballgame for it is her
That I want to visit, just her alone

Well now, I have something to fray my mind
Keep me busy thru the winter opined

Keep Your Wits Then About

I know a spot down by downy grasses
There in a crevice that's so hard to reach
A most wondrous place which one caresses
Then dreams those thoughts of cream and peach

It is restful, relaxing and sleep comes soon
Blankets of leaves cover one's smile resting
And small, furry mammals, surely a boon
Lay then betwixt one's legs safely nesting

Should one dream of love as often happens
Fairies will dance and sing among the leaves
Tossing flowers, for they have no weapons
Still they're jealous of love their Elf believes

Should you stumble upon and find this spot
Keep your wits then about; treasure what's got

KING MILL POND

Where the Cannon is dammed I rest my soul
Countless lovers gazed out their thoughts at ease
Whilst cool breeze did assuage what hurt they'd mull
I let them now comfort my heart to please

It's called King Mill Pond though I know not why
Was there a mill, perhaps when I was young
I can recall a large building did lie
Near the old dam, but that I've guessed, I've sung

Across the pond Bully Wells is larger
It lies on the other side of freeway
And that opens up to Cannon's water
A lake really which hides rivers make way

I hear them now, laughter purls from the gates
Come join with us, the ponds cool and a waits

LADIES LOVE TALES

Fall and garage sales are always in Vogue
It's a cache of useless items of worth
Cast off pointy–toe pumps, maybe a brogue
Use of a compass that only shows north

Sometimes all the neighbors join in around
Then a garage is no longer enough
So the items are placed out on the ground
And it's called a yard sale on the rough

Once in a while treasures are bought cheaply
And there're stories of old Master's paintings
Purchased for ten dollars; seller weeply
When told it was appraised, thousands it brings

I have listened to the banter of sales
More like gossip as then ladies love tales

Lake Mazaska

What is different is there're cabins fronting
The blue lakes now where once before I'd steal
Of view these clear waters where quite daunting
We wouldst skinny dip or fish and boat genteel

This lake west of Faribault was then renowned
For its monster that lurked the deep, dark holes
A cute market ploy of Shieldsville; bemused
Neighbor lakes where no creatures there lolls

The Sioux may have ventured along paths here
Did they fish and hunt, then camp by lakes edge
In this very spot where I've parked my gear
As now their ghosts of past summers allege

Floating by a winsome gal, a boater
She caught my eye, but then didn't loiter

LEAST THE INTENDED MISCONSTRUES

To be a poet must a critic be
That to pass judgment of love's own beauty
Be captious; some might say critical; he
Should be truthful, for that a sworn duty

To each his own I say; but then to me
A poet speaks his heart in rhymed meter
And in the voice of those that wish to be
A Romeo or Juliet tweeter

In romance a poet must be careful
For if his own, then it must be stated
Least the intended misconstrue; tearful
The hurt not meant to her berated

I think I'd enjoy life if an artist
No one's hurt by being a realist

Leaving the Door Open

To the land of little snowfall he came
Bringing glad cheer on this Christmas evening
For twas well known that he would soon acclaim
That this poet speaks, as no one's leaving

For up on this roof top the snows piled high
And looking about then soon would appear
An old frosty esquire seen with a tie
With a grin he proclaimed; Latte my dear

He took but a swallow, then to his lips
His hand made a gesture, throwing a kiss
Then turned towards the doorway making some quips
A fol–de–rol tunes all off–key this Kris

Leaving the door open, loudly we'd hear
Open mike I will return to you next year

LET TEN WORDS THEN ADORN

My heart flutters; sweet words I hear from you
Ten in number, twelve of meter they purl
Had you written hundreds no more would do
Than your heartfelt answer, ten orbs of pearl

For how lovely speaks of beauty or grace
Guileless words there printed, my soul is touched
And I do so desire to share in place
Objects of deep meaning, my Rose thus broached

But tis the last which stirs within of fire
For you have just promised what I've hoped for
To greet once more, our thoughts to then inspire
Of thy painting and my sonnets encore

If I should die before we meet again
Let ten words then adorn my tomb as lain

LET THE GOOD TIMES ROLL

The Trumpet flowers in profuse numbers
Play their fanfare; the breeze then a stirring
Tis a glorious day, not one for slumbers
And I am alive; this feeling recurring

But where are the Sparrows that feed herein
Have they flown to other cafés to steal
From the plates of shoppers found there within
As their life time is spent looking for meal

I'm rather late today for I'd tinker
At home with more IPhone music to load
And the nine poems I typed with no rancor
In fact it was pleasant; poetry flowed

Let the good times roll; words from old time song
Not bad that advice as I move along

Let This Day Mark the Start

I've been trying to think what Will wouldst say
He loved rapture, adored the pull of force
That drew those in love to react this way
He'd no doubt write; "forsake manners, of course"

Then shout thy glee, wakeup all of friendships
Tell them there's free ale and wine for I've sworn
My love to my princess; there be gossips
But from my lips tis true, love this day born

Someone tell Will and he'll write a sonnet
Tis said by few that he writes a fool's tale
But I know him well; he'll get right on it
And pen rhymed words that tells of love's chortle

Let this day mark the start, two lives in bliss
Then send out the Fairies, tell all of this

Let This Greet be Ours

I am dreaming of our kiss when we meet
Shall I guess of its sweetness of taste
Or will it be that warm lush of our greet
When my arms will surround you; ne'er of haste

My dear, your eyes will tell; they are most kind
And shall be like sparkles; dazzled I'll be
As they're telling me of the love I'll find
And mine shall then answer with love fully

Yes, of course we then will be most proper
Though I'd like to be young and not abashed
Making embrace a most amorous tender
Amid much loud clapping; cheers as we dashed

What if I would arrive; freshen allures
Then knock on your door; let this greet be ours

Let You Know of My Longing

Are thou a star twinkling at me tonight
Then from distance tell me, are you quite far
Yet you appear to be brightest in sight
Perhaps blinking like a flashing pulsar

Oh what I'd give to view you up close now
To see your size; are you larger than Earth
Giving warmth to a smaller planet somehow
Or are you just playing with me in mirth

A dark cloud has hidden my view of you
So I'll now go inside; you will observe
Then my absence; duly noted; withdrew
Do you log my absence; saved to preserve

I'll check again on some cloudless evening
Give a wave; let you know of my longing

LETTING THE MOOD COME THROUGH

Lonely times I now spend at night with pen
Only the beat, beat of music keeps me
Going, laying those one–liners here then
Such of megrims I work myself thoroughly

These late years of output; my mind active
Won't last that long, but my sonnets could tell
To think this warms my heart, stays my motive
Penning of poems that soothe, makes love so swell

So what if I labor, surely it's love
That makes me to ponder each thought with care
Wanting for you reader to sense moods of
Tender kissing and sweet embrace so faire

I ask only that you discard my angst
Letting the mood come through thus gives me thanks

LETTING THOSE THAT LOSE LOVE

I have talked of many things that swirl round
Confused your heart; became at once dizzy
Such a smoothie, I have charmed all around
Some left unfilled because I am busy

For they played with danger; I had told them
Warned that this might damage their hearts about
But they were quite willing; life on the rim
Not of boredom but of venture wins out

Oh I am blamed for that is a given
My name taken in vain, perhaps inane
Were it not so easy to ask even
I have them, they clamor now for my name

I am, suppose in a small sense mortal
Letting those that lose love through my portal

Like a Fly on the Wall

Sitting with the artists I felt at home
Except the days color purple not worn
As day before, so it was white as foam
With flag and USA emblem adorn

Mike was doing Van Gogh paintings sketches
He had this book, sort of a quick primer
Van Gogh's paintings, never were there etches
His of oil, Mike's pencil nickel–dimer

All the greatest artists did these drawings
Quickly they'd sketch scenes that later they'd paint
Often the same drawings would bring awing's
From the gallery; prices so high they'd faint

I was like a fly on the wall; hidden
In thought I wrote calmly doing what bidden

LIKE THE CRETAN BULL

I've attempted to write in unrhymed verse
Blundering forward like the Cretan Bull
Yet it reads quite well, the meanings not terse
And gives *raison de plus* to be hopeful

I had thought that I could write more freely
And not have to worry about rhyming
That the lines would flow like warmed up jelly
The taste sugary of lover's pining

Still the form of Shakespeare's finest sonnets
And those I call Keatsean romantic
Reverberate like a nest of hornets
Yet my writings still of the pedantic

Let my poems experience the full gamut
For my heritage of forms quixotic

LIKE WARM FUDGE

Softly she moves against my side of bed
I can feel her fervid, burning body close by
And I'm drawn as the moth to the fire; led
Then to embrace, my leg betwixt her thigh

As she snuggles her head on my shoulder
I rub my hand gently along her spine
And I hear sighs which makes me grow bolder;
Abduct as the Romans did to Sabine

Such then is the pleasure which builds within
And if the gods permit I can finish
With a fanfare, a most joyous bargain
And as Don Juan would say; with a flourish

Spending longish mornings with my Karen
Like warm fudge when it cools, be it harden

LIVING IN THE SOUTHWEST DESERT

Do I detect a breeze blowing my way
Bringing relief from the noon sun glaring
Tis but a huff, sadly a puff, a stray
Whiff of wind that neither cools or airing

Do I see dark clouds there hinting of rain
Or just virga never reaching the ground
I pray that the monsoon surely must deign
Needed moisture and give thunder a sound

Do I feel the effects of my cooler
For I'm blessed with dry air which is godsend
But bring humid air then it's a fooler
And blows warm air and no cooling's append

Living in the southwest desert I find
Every day the weather of talk opined

Look At Us They Declare

Tis the crispness of fall; this October
When winds are spent and rain lingers elsewhere
Then the flowers that bloom; summer's left ov'rs
Show their beauty; look at us they declare

The skies like a painter's gesso light blue
Before he paints a cloud or a sunset
And with mountain's Aspen green leaves adieu
The fall colors turn in shades, then beset

The Black Bear, done gorging on ripe berries
Wobbles towards the fallen tree where its roots
Provide a place to live; there her babies
Will be born when the snow's blanket there puts

I love the fall season's coolness of air
But just around, here comes winter; beware

LOOSE YOUR HEARTSTRINGS

What's it worth I ask, life going lonely
Is there some gauge that says you've had it all
That once it is ended no love poems see
No notes amour, no calls at night befall

And to whom is this owed, this pledge devoid
Of the simplest pleasures of new love dibs
I think not God; then if not him wouldst Freud
Say it was your ego telling you fibs

It is your life and when you're gone who cares
Who will praise your steadfast life so cloistered
For in your heart you yearn for love and dares
To live again, to feel your heart roistered

Then let me aid, become my love once more
Loose your heartstrings, entwine with mine and soar

INTERLUDE OF LOVE

Ode to the French Revolution
(A love story-thirteen sonnets)

Three additional Love poems

Scolding, So French

I saw her, just a glance passing by near
She is a Rose; beauty beyond my words
Where does she go; I run, quick like a deer
Then lose the coach, teeming masses, the hordes

I will wait here again, there now, she comes
And I will jump upon the coach bumping
Riding it to her home, my hearts blood thrombs
If I'm spotted then it's whipping, thumping

The coach stops, I alight, quickly scurry
Behind empty barrels, my views now clear
Then she steps down, oh so dainty she be
And her hair curled and red ribboned appear

Loud, her voice; en retard, scolding, so French
I stand and glare, tis of hatred I wrench

THAT YOUR ACTIONS COVERT

Paul, I rushed back, this mobs getting whipped up
But I caught a coach tail, now there's a tale
In the coach such beauty; gold like syrup
A rose I saw, but then at rest, fatal

For she is the daughter of Emile Veygoux
And a bourgeois known for having close ties
To the royal court at Versailles; a clue
Perhaps if I woo her to learn of lies

For she is not of our ilk, that I'm sure
Hold on Francois, do you know her first name
Yes, I'm told it's Camille, a name most pure
So let me try, at worst I fail this game

I will tell our leaders for they must know
That your actions covert and thus allow

You'll Do What I Say

At the doorway I pulled on the bell chain
The maid took one look; for service back door
But I want...the door slammed and then came rain
I stood dumbfound, the rain began to pour

Psst, a small boy signaled to me; come here
Why not I thought, perhaps I get shelter
He led; soaked I followed, knowing not where
This is my hide, father built it for her

And who is her, I asked simply to know
Why my sister, Camille, but she's grown-up
So now it is mine and welcomes my foe
For I have you under arrest, tied up

My name; Marshall Davout; you'll be Dessaix
A French General and you'll do what I say

Comes Now Blithely

Tell me Marshall Davout about Camille
Let's not talk of her, don't you want to play
I'd like to but really let's wait until...
The rain now stopped, I said; mustn't delay

As I started to leave he grabbed my coat
I can tell you about Camille, where she takes walk
Marshall, Sir I'm in debt; of her I dote
If what you say is true, later we'll talk

That night I saw Paul and made my report
She walks alone each morn by the Seine
I will make a ruse to allow rapport
Invite her to café, I'll use my brain

The sun was up, birds were singing brightly
And there she is again; comes now blithely

And Love Wouldst Keep

Thoughts came running through my brain as I slept
Betwixt of love and my duty to fight
I was tearing my heart in two ways kept
And love was now winning its way this night

I shall devise this plan; drop my text books
As I approach her, feint stumbles, hopeless
And she will stop to help me, see my looks
Then we'll laugh and feel gay, not now hapless

I'll tell her the café Montmartre is close
There we will sip some wine, chatting at ease
I'll feel her out, learn of her views, her boasts
Charm this beauty, learn her secrets, release

My ruse thought through, perhaps I shall now sleep
As my heart was beating, thus love wouldst keep

Do You Know Me

I shant now be nervous, recall my ruse
For I have planned complete, just let it be
Oh my heavens, she passed me, I shall lose
My plan is not gotten; halt there I plea

As if by saints action she then sat down
I took a step closer, then just stood there
Do you want some money, she asked me sound
No, you see...books tumbled to her feet bare

I bent down to pick them up as did she
And our foreheads bumped which caused her to fall
Quickly then I cradled her head warmly
Her eyes flickered, then starred taking in all

Are you injured Camille I asked sincere
Do you know me, how come my name I hear

His Sad Story of the Rain

I thought fast; I recall your name spoken
But you are not injured, that bump nasty
No, but perhaps I should sit here broken
As your books ruined my shoe clasp most lastly

Look, this clearly was my fault; let it be
I'll help you up, maybe we walk about
That won't be required sir, I can stand quite free
But then again she swooned; his arms reached out

Francois helped her to the café nearby
Ordered then two brandies for both were shocked
Camille's color returned as they sat nigh
My names Francois, I must explain my act

He told of coach ride and meeting Marshall
His sad story of the rain, his ruse; all

THIS MOST HECTIC DAY

Camille sat there quiet; Francois looked glum
I think I should like to go home now, please
No need for you to call a coach to come
I will walk back, my minds now quite at ease

Francois rose and said; I'll walk back with you
No, please do not tangle this mess further
Father would not look with favor here too
It is best not recall this meet either

With that Camille left him standing alone
His chest fallen, all he could do was watch
Then in distance were heard gunshots, now known
And my Camille's path, the soldiers will catch

This most hectic day now becomes nightmare
Francois must stop her, take Camille for care

Battles Waged in Paris

Halt, who goes there, soldiers checking papers
Francois then saw Camille waiting in line
He grabbed her arm, quickly, these aren't neighbors
Camille yelled, let go of me now, I'm fine

No, I won't let go, there's fighting ahead
The King will be taken, and so will friends
But I must reach father, his life I dread
Come, there's a way around, my cloak appends

Through some alleys, Francois led his Camille
Here, crawl under this fence, we'll take this hide
I know this place, Brother Louis hides well
Francois, I hear soldiers, we should abide

Throughout the night battles waged in Paris
And brave Francois held her from its harass

He Was Robespierre's Spy

Francois stirred first, Camille lay by asleep
Camille, he said softly, there's no gun fire
It should be safe now but make not a peep
As we enter your home what might transpire

Louis, exclaimed Camille; where is father
Hello Dessaix, I see you've met Camille
Louis, his names Francois; answer brother
He was taken last night; Louis looked ill

Francois spoke; most likely taken to jail
I can find out, then come back with more word
But tell me truth Camille, or I might fail
Was your father close to the King's accord

Camille, much grave her looks, replied; no sir
He was Robespierre's spy, a friend most ever

Captured by Our Frondeurs

May I say a word here; Louis then asked
By all means, said Francois, I need guidance
One of father's takers I heard says; masked
Does that mean they weren't real soldiers at glance

If they were masked, then I submit a trick
Tell me why so Francois, said staid Camille
As your father is aiding our cause they'd pick
His men masked to fool your neighbors as well

If this is the case and I'm sure it is
Then your father will be meant to appear
Captured by our Frondeurs, his role complice
And thus again be most useful to peer

I think you and Louis will be safe now
As our leaders will guard his home I'll vow

A Last Kiss, Then Goodbye

I must leave now, much has to be done here
I will make sure guards are posted close too
So I bid now adieu; please shed no tear
Camille for I love you, my life's with you

Louis, please stay here; I'll escort Francois
Both then walked to the front gate, then they paused
Camille looked at Francois, then kissed him, ah...
And then for each rapture and bliss was caused

I shant let you leave me, please stay I pray
I can't Camille, I must report to fight
But I will soon return, give me a day
If I'm not then able, a note I'll write

A last kiss, then goodbye as love parted
Francois was killed, shot by sniper, martyred

But I Like My Ending

You may well ask, for the question lingers
Why have Francois killed when love was starting
Mainly the odds favored death palled zingers
And so many fell, the bodies carting

I could have made him a hero and lived
But then the more utile reason might be
Francois's social standing; much less he give'd
As fair Camille was of class and money

But I like my ending, it is so French
Like La Bohème, Andrea Chénier; love ends
And death makes these poignant endings a cinch
Perhaps a play or a novel unbends

I'll bet with some genus one could name stars
To play the leads in this movie; "Martyrs".

LOVE CONQUERS WITH FORCE

Let my love then travel as from afar
To reach your heartstrings there plucked by me
Doth your heart then tremble, can'st I then bare
All my fervent passion forthwith to thee

Should your heart be stoic; my plea refused
And in defense of love shutout implores
Thence a prisoner of your heart twas bemused
And find your wall daunting to my explores

I shall like Troy thence siege withal my might
Until I find your hearts weakness hidden
And with ladders and ram break through with fight
To claim my prize, your heart thus there bidden

Let it be said that love conquers with force
That no stronghold can then resist of course

ONCE MY GESTE IN ORDER

Thou throw words with venom stinging squarely
Your eyes pierce my defense which I've composed
Shall I wave my white flag, ask for parley
For the result wouldst be against supposed

I shall retreat; fear yet I will return
With new armor which will deflect your scorn
And stout cannons to pound away in turn
Wearing you down until a breach is torn

Then in triumph with all bugles blaring
I will enter to claim as prize your heart
And all the love goest with it glaring
For I will tame you or render apart

Let no battle or fight dampen my ardor
I shall prevail once my geste in order

Taken When Let

Two poems I've penned of love's fiercest conflict
As if in fight a heart is won or lost
But this is not ardent love to inflict
For love is most joyous, always we boast

Let's not rail love spoken but voice whispers
As love needs no cone–shaped device to speak
Simply mouth in mime; I love you; answers
And with a smile sincere let your thoughts leak

Oh thou sweetened of fine clover in lust
Find there Bees who will gather pollen
Then to their hive make of honey as must
Storing sugared combs whence then are stolen

Thy love is not taken away by threat
For it only can be taken when let

CR   CR   CR

LOVE THEN ANON

Oh such sweetness; I find it hard to leave
These nights of close nearness; yet we must so
As her eye is mending; thus we believe
And pray through these moments that we go slow

I shall pour my heart out, telling of lore
For I have no secrets I would not share
It feels strange; yet marvel at her quest for
All my exploits, things she never would dare

I have become a much better lover
More so in my caring of her tender
Just to lie in blissful warmth for ever
Tis this love so grand; I bask in wonder

I am like a river; flowing along
Never being used up; love then anon

Love to Explain

While I wait for you all pleasure's on hold
And the world seems quite drab while love's apart
But I know that you'll soon be here I'm told
With kiss of such rapture warming my heart

I've made my life's choices; all are with you
So no use I pretend that it's other
For my face is a give away; tis true
I am open as a book, my love here

I will wait for you; the time flows on by
Because in the ending my prize thus won
Is your essence, your pure heart to lie
Next to mine as I clasp you to me done

Never did I think of waiting as pain
Until, that is, I had love to explain

LOVER'S FOOD

I think I understand it; this feeling
My drifting off in daydreams; thoughts of you
It's so peaceful staring at the ceiling
Watching the shadows; seeing what they do

Let me have my reverie, it's so peaceful
Listening to a voice murmur songs of love
Afloat on gentle waves sinusoidal
I'm lulled to sleep, soft cooing's like the dove

I think God gave us each special moments
To clear our minds of daily thoughts of toil
Sweeping those cobwebs; minor rudiments
Starting afresh; markedly jovial

I'm awake now and in a joy filled mood
Wonderful this call from you; lover's food

LOVE'S BUT A THORN

I've dreamt what comes in the Fall's late season
When leaves then turn into colors orange
And Morning Glory's late blooms a blazon
Where now the morning sunshine rays do tinge

And here sits my Helen; in her glory
Her eyes not at me; Zeus has taught her well
She seeks someone younger that's con amore
Who'll love her in earnest and not pell–mell

Shall I pray to Venus; invoke her help
To have mercy on men; those who are low
That wants friendship only; wishing to chelp
As their motives laurel; asking then ergo

I'm now wakened in the sunlight this morn
My dream is but memory; love's but a thorn

LUCKY THE GIRL YOU CATCH

True love is like skiing on the mountain
Once you're committed and on your way downhill
There's no going back to the start again
You might pause or fall but finish you will

Such then is in marriage this vow contract
And though you may take spills; make not a peep
Dust the snow off and then resume your track
For you're in need until death makes you weep

Few are given; call it second chance here
But when it does happen accept this bliss
As a new race; but still having rules where
You can then be made to forfeit success

The downhill race is quite a treat to watch
Don't fall as is lucky the girl you catch

Lulling You in Norse Lore

I want you to know the pleasure I seek
Is found in my being with you always
Whether it is in walking along a creek
Or a pathway being lit by sun's rays

I am content to sit for hours with you
Holding your hands; rubbing you in comfort
Or just watching you paint sunset's rich hue
Let me become then your private pilot

For I then shall protect you from all harm
Become your close wingman; ne'er out of place
But tucked in tight; ready my guns to arm
To then engage all foes; become your Ace

But best of all, to read to you my poems
Lulling you in Norse lore; telling of Gnomes

MAKING MISSTEPS

I told her faire maiden of my ardor
To which she did reply of no concern
So I sent her bouquets of Corn Flower
Now she sneezes; oh why could I not learn

Then to the Fair, together hand–in–hand
I pitched the ball and won a green ribbon
But in the light rain the color did ran
And left an ugly smear on her apron

Then we paused on the bridge to view the ducks
And I gave her a crust of bread to feed
Tis mold on it she cried; now that's me lucks
A Baker's daughter, why me Lord mislead

For I'm but a simple poet in love
Making missteps like those mentioned above

Marked Me For Service

Is there kinship, thus the far north beckoned
Come join with me it cries, for blood reminds
We to recall those fierce battles reckoned
As you the seed of past portent consigns

You have no draw on me to speak of old
For I'm loyal to this country thence born
And what of my talent, has it been told
Of the broadsword, the axe, a shield thus worn

No, I'll not fight wars that harken back here
I may be your kinsman, but look further
There are plenty of fools willing to bear
Knives in combat, these men fought with Arthur

They'll not leave me alone, my fame once known
Has marked me for service I'll not condone

Marriage is Shared

To my way of thinking, marriage is shared
In parts equal; both the good and the bad
You can't just take the good ones, the rest pared
And piled on your partner; common this fad

Oh there will be swerving, some say; bending
Of the ratio other than half and half
And if that then occurs with some rending
Look to soothe, to slake, to laugh with distaff

There is much to be said about meting
For it involves trusting love to do best
And if this is missing in one's treating;
Either party is then without what's blest

Making then your union wondrous in bliss
Is quite simple; share the pie as gratis

Mind Wander

I let my mind wander among the stars
Was I being starry-eyed this dark night
For the vastness of those empty light years
Made me perpend things of little or slight

Unless Einstein was wrong, only visions
Of the cosmos that I'll see for certain
Are through my eyes, as space travel prisons
My trip ventures; they're too tiny for gain

Why then has God made this cosmos boundless
Am I being told in a subtle way then
That all answers aren't found on the surface
But found listening to my heartbeats within

Perhaps I will never have full insight
As my mind is of the poet tonight

More So the Great Deluge

Thunder and then the rain came down pouring
But then some five minutes later it stopped
And now I can hear it again whoring
As it beckons the dry grass to drink sopped

Oh it temps us this great crier of tears
With its pittance of moist wetness that comes
As I dream of rivers flowing through weirs
To quench the dry crops thirst, soaking the loams

Weather people say a cold front then nears
And highs on the morrow will be reduced
A most welcome event; the front endears
To all of us that have waited hung noosed

Rather simple is the rainfall I feel
More so the great deluge that I might steal

More Space I Wish

We sang duets that much I do recall
And I wasn't gallant, my mind elsewhere
But now I fear I may have missed withal
That spark that ne'er became a flame to wear

Sixty years, is that too long in memory
Or does song live ageless to then explore
What not tries in vocal impulse sensory
To yet obtain what once may have been lore

We have skirted at the edge; such dancing
That now reminds me of witty reply
And I wonder should I now be lancing
Or let it lay; my mind needs help I cry

This fine sonnet I find hard to finish
What I have said requires more space I wish

Moscow Memories

Was it your eyes, Russian Moscow eyes there
Hinting of held secrets never revealed
When I looked, just for a second, did bare
Of love absent but then it was gone, sealed

Then you came back; normal, your smile complete
And I figured I had misjudged you feigned
Brimming with pour rire you answered then sweet
Giving me of allure your facts thus gained

When I told you about Anna you perked
Did you know this Russian singer of note
So I went and got her CD; I'd parked
Close by, you then entered her name by rote

I thought then that perhaps sonnets would cheer
Bring back Moscow Memories you hold most dear

Anna
Netrebko – Russian Album
2006 Deutsche Grammophon B0008153–02
Feigned –not genuine or real
Pour rire – not to be taken seriously – for laughing

MULTI-HATTED

When the Black Cat opened its doors this morn
I gave a sigh; now we poets can meet
As this is our home base, where poems adorn
The shelves in the backroom, so take a seat

Then next Sunday being ninth of month
Poets will meet and read at most three poems
All done in a round–the–room reading romps
Where light applause greets them that do yeoman's

I've not noticed any changes made here
The books remain as they were in late June
So it was what Rhonda promised back there
To get away, relax, look at the moon

Then too, poets came in and we chatted
About our life, teaching, multi–hatted

My Choosing of Worth

When I hear your voice my heart swells near burst
And fuzzy tingling's scamper up and down
I'm immune to pain; Bee is that your worst
If I stumble, soft landings tumble–down

I'm like my butter, soft and moldable
Putty to your fingers; I acquiesce
To make a change, you find that I'm turnable
And when I see you smile I effloresce

But in honesty I'm quite adamant
When asked if I would give up everything
To follow my heart, to woo endearment
And the answer, a resounding bidding

I have but this life to live now on Earth
So don't fault me in my choosing of worth

My Cosset

Ah my cosset, time now passes so quick
Had we but a lifetime what bliss there be
We would stroll the forest; leaves we would pick
To press them in scrapbooks, our own memory

We could float high aloft; heated balloon
Drifting this way and that, pending the wind
Or ride on the Zephyr, fly to Kowloon
Take a steamer to where ever, our end

Yet we rest now, comfort at last is ours
To spend time with scion, so fast they grow
Then paint and write homage; ivory towers
That we use to escape, daydreams we sow

I call you my little lamb, my cosset
Tis what Bard of Avon would write; abet

My Faire Soul Asking

My most precious jewel that outshines the sun
Whose grand lustre pales the finest diamond
I have found you fairly, my prize thus won
As you're my sole passion, ne'er I remand

I give a love–story; chanson d'amour
To cheer your soul, to wish for love always
And I will be there with you, ever more
Oh my love, so much my heart cries out praise

Listening to the greatest love songs, romance,
And the best–loved duets cause goose–bumps now
And my heart beats soundly liken a dance
That throws petti–coats and tails to bellow

Let this moment go on, never suspend
My faire soul asking it not to end

My Love In It

Let there be no doubt in my love of thee
Though it has lain dormant for all these years
A spring rain has nourished this seed to be
A strong sapling which now outgrows his peers

Deep down I'm most loving; my roots are deep
And will anchor me thus steadfast for you
We will stand as our fore parents and reap
From the prairie those strengths garnered there too

And in the fall my fruit ripened you eat
It is sweet and filling; slowly you glow
As my warmth now enters; within the heat
Swells your heart, you become lovesome I know

Let my poems fly to you as this sonnet
That you can read in bed; my love in it

My Mind Wonders

As I lay here breathing, my mind wonders
Of the billions or more that went before
Did they wonder too of daydreamed splendors
Of things in life knowing, wishing, yet poor

Of course they did, yet few would write them down
Content to let their word go round and round
But had they done, I will wager a crown
We'd be better off had their thoughts been bound

Often in dream land when the mood suits me
I think about the stars so far distant
Perhaps too a Stone Age lad had fondly
Gazed in wonder like me; shared this instant

We will never know, at least I think so
What those thoughts contained many years ago

My Most Wondrous Feline

Sometimes I think she just doesn't love me
When I see those starring eyes, her look stern
I might as well go to bed; act sleepy
For the time will come soon that she'll return

Then to snuggle up like nothing happened
For her hurts short lived; for that I'm thankful
And in the morn I feel love not dampened
She goes about her day like her pails full

I don't have a teeming number of friends
So just one that's angry with me bothers
I'll try my best; I don't want to reach ends
Call me coward, I shant mind the others

I hold her most special this cat of mine
For she's Twinkie, my most wondrous feline

My Poem Liked Roundly

Your calls mean so much to me Mon âme
My heart gets a jolt; I'm alive again
And I can write sonnets; love songs to thee
And end my day upbeat as I intend

These calls may be brief but they remain fast
As you drift off to sleep and then settle
Into your dreaming thoughts where I am cast
As your Prince in romance with proved mettle

I am a part of your life from now on
Ne'er to ever leave you; always beside
In person or when I'm away, in song
Lyrics which cheer you, gladden there inside

Oh I cherish you; my heart beats soundly
And I can rest now, my poem liked roundly

My Quests I Pick

Do I spar with love, feint a mock blow near
Confuse those that appose reckless advance
If so then let critics judge my manner
As those pursued lay still their voices askance

Say love is a game, what score doth settle
And do fouls add or just subtract of points
I wouldst not let sudden death then mettle
With the outcome as then it's God's anoints

But let us not squabble; love is freelance
Abides no rules and spurns umpires rulings
Let each in turn resolve their fights of dance
Quick steps are the footwork dueling's

I do not play or spar, I just revel
My quests I pick and not on the level

My Ruby Saloon

Aye, there is that picture over the bar
You're sure now I wouldn't buy if wasn't
Long legs stretched out with a blanket so far
Well it's modest but some parts it doesn't

Tell me about her legs, are they quite white
They're like Ivory with toes pinkish I'd say
And the rest, please tell me more of the sight
Sunlight highlights, I'm sure patrons will pay

Is there red like rubies; oh I like red
It's the darkest kind like wine most pure
And the blanket; a shawl, covers her head
But don't worry, the best parts I ensure

Then let me seal the deal; I'll wire money
I'll call it my Ruby Saloon, sonny

My Thoughts Run of Love

Ever that I write my thoughts run of love
Always will I whisper of sweet words meant
Never false my statements I've made thereof
In truth I do adore you, love thus sent

My pulse quickens when I think of our tryst
That on morrow I'll rush into your arms
And kiss gladly, even madly at first
Then brush lightly my lips, oh how it warms

Then we'll stroll, arm and arm along the Thames
Watching Geese and Ducks as they come landing
To splash then make chatter like young gamines
And laugh as you ask, then the bread crumbs fling

In rest now my sweet dreams present anew
Those of joy and repose thinking of you

My Thoughts Worth Keeping

Sometimes she looks at me, smiles with eyes closed
And I do the same as if we're of minds
That thinks of thoughts that are alike, supposed
But that's nonsense, I must erase these binds

But the thought bears heavy on my conscience
And I shouldn't think like this, not at all
Does she wonder the same; again nonsense
My minds adrift now and out of control

I'll not look back, forget that she is there
Listen to my music, condense my thoughts
Paying of heed to my sonnet with care
Now then I'm more settled of the naughts

I glance at her again, but she's sleeping
And I too feel tired, my thoughts worth keeping

MYSTIC POTION

Deep now within my heart there lays this ode
Of our Norsk blood that by birthright we claim
Which then becomes Thor and Inga's abode
That from Norway to the west shores they came

I feel, oh the wonder they must have had
Of their going to this land of omen
How Thor became the craftsman; so glad
That his Inga was revered by all women

That there is a linkage with real life here
I do not doubt; our lives entwined you see
There is likely magic in the air where
Ever our paths lead; Fairies have made it be

What is real and what is fancy notion
It must tie in with some mystic potion

Ne'er Be Alleged

That I love you; never can there be doubt
For you're the stars, the moon, I view in sight
And the sweetness of fruit lying about
But most of all, what I've dreamt of at night

Those I savor as now recalled from thoughts
And in daydreams relive the bliss thereof
Your touch is all that is missing of broughts
Beggars can't be choosers when they're in love

To be with you is my only intent
And it pains me greatly to feel concern
As you wrestle with your heartstrings hellbent
This way and that; love you give, I discern

Recall then as proof shown, my love I pledge
And not what would anger; ne'er be alleged

NE'ER WOULD LOVE LINK

We sat around inside the house that day
I can recall you were on the settee
Sort of in the middle living room bay
You were barefoot and our meeting; not glee

I think you talked about going out East
Perhaps then you gave me back my picture
The one when I was just two; quite the least
Of my concerns of course; thoughts a mixture

Funny, but now maybe it was terms end
As there were no other sisters about
You might have then mentioned Bill; but not pinned
But it was all over; my fault I'd vote

Had we dated, remained in touch I think
Our life would have ended; ne'er would love link

Nesting in Posh Splendor

At the close of your day fortune passed by
Whence it came from and to thither it goes
It's not telling for this gal prone to lie
She seeks those that gamble, such men she knows

Do not feel sad, luck was never a friend
Some said he was engaged with Miss fortune
That would be a pairing you'd want to wend
To be ensnared and feel wanting of rune

For with magic you'd have no need of skill
And all fortune would then amass of coin
And you would then be heard to say as Will
All's well that ends well, or just pass the wine

Mystic nights in rustic place I'll be
Nesting in posh splendor, fortune and me

All's Well that Ends Well, play by William Shakespeare

Never Get My Work Done

I walked between the stones marking old graves
And heard the cries of lost souls here yelling
Pray there sir, hear my plea, my love ave's
From there across the field; what's he telling

Pay no allure to this hussy asking
She's a widow and he's married thank God
But I wouldst like favor of this tasking
My head stone has fallen and needs of sod

Hush you two now; this man is our digger
He'll soon right all tombstones, cut grass shorter
I'd then request some fresh flowers bigger
Ones that stand tall, perhaps a vase order

I've heard these rants before, tis best I shun
Their pleas else I'd never get my work done

NEVER SAY PASS

I could say I love you many more times
But the day has only twenty–four hours
There's not nearly enough sonnets of rhymes
Or of verse in meter that my heart pours

I could send you bushels of Rose flowers
And pounds of dark chocolate smothered in rum
But soon you'd be wishing that the bowers
Of Rose flowers would hold sweets that taste yum

I could be with you this night in our bed
If our morals were loosened; that won't happen
Even though we wish it might; so we've waited
To make it all above board and open

I won't permit stalemates or an impasse
I will fight for your love; never say pass

Now Unknownst and Rife

They have given me a short time to write
How I wish the ink in my pen endless
So that I could nurture this, hold in sight
My love pouring forth to you most boundless

Oh what can I pen now that will enthrall
Perhaps the trips we took when cares vanished
And the laughter of Mink frolics recall
Then those tender nights when worry banished

That I loved you deeply, of that no doubt
And we had so many years that we shared
That builds our strong castle, our own redoubt
Where we are safe, our thoughts, all those we cared

Don't blame the Crown for I forfeit my life
To save those brave men now unknownst and rife

OF MY TRUEST ACTION

I have often spoken of true friendships
Ones that includes fondness, love and candor
But there are false friendships using just quips
Of words amorous, that use guile and pander

Oh how I wish that my poems ring of truth
That they shout of lasting for all through time
Alas, the lines I write are mine forsooth
They hint what stays within my heart of rhyme

When I speak of friendships and there's a few
Of those, ne'er a waiver; I was steadfast
My life I'd give; 'twere an option most true
And of my quick critics; well, I'd outlast

Say what you please but I'll never give slip
Of my truest action; that of friendship

OF PRINCELY MANNER

You are my Rose flower; essence of life
For your petals enfold, protect the core
That small region to which Bumble Bees rife
With their borrowed pollen come to explore

I shant let the forces of cruel nature
Weather away these robes that now adorn
In such splendor and grace as you mature
Into the sunburst image as if just born

Oh my beauty, wouldst thou bloom for ever
Letting me fill my heart with your bouquet
I will dance of joy; my heart of fervor
Till I can rest in peace at the close of day

Let the Yellow Rose then fly my banner
To be carried high; of princely manner

Old Buckhorn Bar

They tore it down, some said it was unsafe
And there was that façade that fell on down
Could have hurt a passing tourist or waif
But I feel it was the zoning downtown

So now it's gone, empty space there waiting
Is that worse than it was before I ask
Like a gapping toothed mouth, the space grating
To my eye I suppose; maybe a mask

On the back wall someone had drawn figures
And it wasn't until the walls had gone
That the message, colored orange ligures
Spoke of the gem jacinth, but I had none

Is this how it dies; to slowly crumble
The space decay spreading as walls tumble

On Valnt'ine's Day

For all lovers who came this day, pay heed
There is much to ponder when love is felt
So then gather around while I proceed
To tell in my sonnet this gift then dealt

Oh love is a blessing one makes with choice
To woo of a partner; this done with grace
Then deep in your bosom comes this rejoice
Of such glowing splendor shown on your face

You'll walk thus on tip–toe; as if on air
And such dangers present that would surround
They shant not then bother, nor would they dare
You'd smite them with kindness, leave them dumbfound

I give then a promise; tuck this away
Give thanks to your loved one on Valnt'ine's day

One–Liners Most Bold

Every night when sleep has captured love's trove
And thoughts random, stirring within my head
Then moved each way, trying to make sense of
I am open to things natural instead

This is when new content enters my mind
Maybe you know where it comes from; tell me
Or is it a secret; ne'er then I find
Answers that will placate; let my soul be

But if you told; wouldn't trust be broken
And I would have to think of new phrases
There then being little warrant spoken
And my poems lay dead; as blind man gazes

I shant therefore kill the goose that lays gold
But wake each morn with one–liners most bold

ONLY THE WORSE

Didst thou recall when the Fairies came here
Oh, such the fuss it was too; bear in mind
These were English and not of our veneer
But they settled in quite nicely affined

I am afraid I have bad news to tell
Speak up man, but before, give me a pint
As your ale will soften what comes pell–mell;
Is it the elves; has there been a complaint

There has been a murder in the salt fens
Someone we know or were it a stranger
It was Eireen, queen of the elves and kin's
Has there been an arrest; is there danger

This is trouble, do you fear much impact
Only the worse, we've seized your son in fact

Only to Wake and Think

These are moments when my heart starts to ache
What brings these pains on I can but give clues
It might be just music causing heartbreak
Or then again, watching sunsets adieus

In the doldrums; a word of such meaning
To those sailors crossing the vast oceans
It meant slack winds; the ships passage floating
Like I view love's memories in slow motions

Then a fresh breeze will blow away these thoughts
And my journey resumes in glad fashion
I write sonnets; a child's poem that cavorts
And some love poems with once again passion

Then to bed for my day has been time worn
Only to wake and think once more love's forlorn

OUR LOVE NOW REBORN

Memories we leave in the past best unsaid
As we probe in hope to relive full sum
Love most brief in time; yet cautious we tread
For it was a preview of love to come

Then "The first time ever I saw your face"
As I borrow those words; Eastwood's loves treat
I knew then one day there would be a place
For loves renewal; made the circle complete

My love is blind of those memories gone by
As sight is now showing our loves so fine
While I bask in wonder of your lithe sigh
For it sends warm shivers down my bare spine

These months apart build our solid resolve
That our love now reborn new will evolve

Lyrics from Ewan MacColl
The First Time Ever I Saw Your Face

OUR LOVE SO PERFECT

I could give you diamonds, even gold; pearls
But none would match my poems written hereof
Such amour, that within my heart unfurls
And waves Eros' banner telling of love

Let me bewitch you with poems of romance
Entice you to unheard–of sheer rapture
Leaving you here floating as in a trance
Till I gently coax you back to capture

Thus I enfold you with my arms around
Never to let you go; this I promise
And should danger approach; menace and hound
I will protect you; thus ne'er be remiss

I give fully to you my pledge written
That our love so perfect, ever bidden

Our Sunday Chit-Chats

I look forward to our Sunday chit-chats
Both of us so busy, our own time outs
When each of us relate of this and that's
Of our worlds events, our where abouts

When you stop and think, this really is small
Compared to the hundred sixty-seven
Hours that remain in a week, is that all
Yet it makes up in full time lost even

I might wonder what will be made of this
When in later years my readers will ask
What did they talk about; oh, let them guess
Never in a million years lift our mask

Really I could care less what is inferred
It will no doubt be wrong, stupid and erred

Our Wait We have Endured

Oh God I do so love her most dearly
For she makes my heart pause when she comes near
And at dawn when wakened; is it early
No, no; hold me closely whispered in ear

When we're walking I will offer my arm
Open the car door and assist with chair
Little things that is not expected; but warm
Her smile, and I rise to heights wouldst I dare

I can sit for hours just writing a poem
While she wanders about doing her things
Poignant my thoughts, never be they lonesome
For she is most wondrous in all she brings

There's much to be thankful for as endowed
Our wait we have endured is now allowed

Paint with Dark Colors

Did love of me lessen as time passed by
Because I feel your love now faint memory
Has this August been worse than was July
Much like the essence of your home's flowe'ry

I watched the sun settling; slowly fading
Getting smaller with time; then one day, gone
And thought; that is just where my love's heading
Like Glen Campbell's farewell leaving Tucson

Yet I'm sanguine; the sun will rise again
Though my life as poet has ups and downs
This fact gives me reason to hope. Amen
Then let me bask in self–assured pronouns

Perhaps I tend to paint with dark colors
Those of image that I think as dolors

Passion is Quite Basic

Give then of your reading done when night falls
Letting sonnets warm the coolness of love
Perhaps a phrase in rhyme to cheer withal's
Or of meter pleasing in its write of

Your heart perhaps heavy in thoughts of rue
Then find this poem comfort in your sorrow
Forswear revenge, dismiss acts of issue
Instead give love renewed on the morrow

If of folly then ask forgive this soul
Swear of heart that promise is now given
And with a gift cement of your new role
For if this loves of worth then all's even

Oh there are then plenty that wear your shoes
Passion is quite basic, let love infuse

PEN MY POEM LAST TONIGHT

Today I stayed in my pajamas all day
In the morning I went outside to feed
My birds and saw a pest had cut its way
Through my newly planted shrub as if weed

Then I ate my lunch with Twinkie watching
But the chicken and cheese sandwich wasn't
On her menu so I ate while catching
The news, but that bored me; not all pleasant

Took a nap then watched a vampire movie
Had my dinner sans blood of course; then went
To bed to write three more stanza; groovy
Because I was still in pajamas there sent

Thus in one–half hour I'll call you; then write
My e–mail and pen my poem last tonight

Perhaps a B.L.T.

Inside because of rain; the yard chairs wet
And it's cool, temps dropping to low sixties
Funny how all this can change what is met
At the Happy Belly Deli nifties

Mike's got his sketch pad out, flowers again
Pinks and yellows and wow, orange petals
But then artists as are poets most fain
Leaving those that view their works in riddles

Mandy opened the wide window towards street
Letting the cool air in; where has it been
But I welcome its flow, oh what a treat
Wafting the smells of the tempest now seen

All of this has gotten my taste buds piqued
Perhaps a B.L.T. will get me tweaked

Perhaps It Was Wrong

I hurt, but I feel her pain now instead
And I tremble; I feel my heart shaking
This shall not go away; no rest in bed
Will make me feel better; her grief making

I call upon my guise; soft words spoken
To then convey my heart's plea, now contrite
That I will; I must show change betoken
I pledge to God ever to do what's right

My heart sacrificed to make her's better
If that means I forfeit mine, so be it
As all of her torment is my fetter
Chained to my soul as was Marley's to wit

Lord, was my sin only that I loved strong
From her point of view, perhaps it was wrong

Playing Rural Fairs

It's all done with mirrors the man explained
You know, the hands faster than your eyes see
But how can that be; it can't be sustained
For he will drown surely, no air there be

Just you watch now; in a minute...voila!
And up he raised breaking surface with splash
See now, the Great Merlin, you view with awe
Submerged for one-half hour; he has panache

Jimmy, get me a dry towel; quickly
That lad's asking questions; I say we go
But the second shows sold out, must we flee
If they find out our con it's the hoosegow

Sideshows were quite common after the War
Playing rural fairs they were cheats by far

PLAYING WITH YOUR CAT IN BED

I threw a wad; it was paper and bounced
Then in a high arched pounce, Twinkie attacked
Catching the wad with claws, she then announced
Do it again; I did, the wad she whacked

This was a fun game played; show–off moment
Of her prowess; she was a good mouser,
As yet labeled; for the skill not cogent,
But she would plead inbred; I'm the closer

Now she lies tucked in; all fours are covered
And with eyelids closing, sort of smirking
She knows I have now been bested, cowered
And no longer willing to play; irking

So the moral of this story is this
Playing with your cat in bed; might ruin bliss

Please Guide Me to My Love

The sun and the moon find me no solace
Those orbs of time that have of fame lasting
Wouldst I champ'n of such heave'nly premise
When though as not mortal, they've failed to bring

Simply I will build on chance of the roll
For the odds are better, although the house
Is most favored; still, I bet my bankroll
And should I lose; destined thence to poorhouse

Doth thou not trust Eros of fair Venus
Have they failed you; why then thrust them aside
As the path you now choose becomes runeless
Let me set up a tryst; there to confide

God or goddess, please guide me to my love
And I'll enshrine ever you my votive

PLIGHTED TROTH AND RAPTURE

You came into my life like a firestorm
Caught me off–guard; turned me upside–down too
My world was a topsy–turvy transform
Where up was down; oh it was quite the coup

But you gave me time to reclaim balance
It was then that I knew your worth to me
That our life was destined for great brilliance
Which would lead to pleasure, gladness and glee

Karen my love; the moon and stars appear
In their glory when you're near me at night
I hear the toads croaking; no snakes I fear
And the nighthawks dive and turn in dogfight

You are my one–in–a–million capture
That holds me in plighted troth and rapture

Puss of Mine

How dare you leave me here cried puss of mine
Shut up without a bed decent for cat
And the water was warm, full of sea brine
Least you forgot, kitty litter has scat

And one more thing; dog food is not cat food
It has allured creatures one might call dogs
That is if they had tails and they smelled good
But these mongrels are from a swamp of frogs

Are you listening to me human being
For I detect a slight snicker suppressed
So don't think I won't file complaint seeing
Your crass posture against felines addressed

There is really little I can add here
As the Supreme Court hears appeal this year

QUAIL BAKED WITH THYME

My good friend Bard let us partake of ale
Tis my treat, no, of that I'll not abate
Then let me ply of your wisdom local
Does name of pub Wild Boar recall of late

Oh, so you know of it, good let's make haste
There to meet friends and a tale be told
And so we went, twas not far, our walk paced
The Wild Boar was crowded, the hour not old

I scanned the faces but none answered of rote
So we took a table just near the door
Perhaps they are detained elsewhere I note
So let us eat Quail baked with thyme therefore

Had my friends came then of poems tale appear
Not of other poet, but by Shakespeare

QUEEN OF COUNTY ARMAGH

From the hill he looked down; ah, there she is
Her hair scarlet like the berry of Yew
And now she is running, a game it tis
For no young boy will catch her, that he knew

Queen of County Armagh, she'd reign this year
He'd seen her with garlands of white flowers
And at first thought a crown; princess she were
But no, she were a lass of green bowers

He had noticed her there with fresh cuttings
Perhaps she sold them at county market
He would buy a bouquet tied with yarn strings
Then ask her name; praying that he shant fret

That this was the girl he would wed someday
He had no doubt as he began his way

Rapture Abodes in Smiles

From your heart dear, I beg that you forgive
For I have but sorely given of love
Too much has my ardor been my motive
And not the deep friendship that you spoke of

How one fixes love is never easy
And to repair broken hearts takes longer
I'll start with the tenet; you've been busy
And build support to make this bond stronger

Then for sustained love I pledge less passion
For we have shown rapture abodes in smiles
And in reading poems when they're in fashion
These then of true romance and not beguiles

Even if for ever, I will perdure
And I'll prove to you that I'm worth amour

Rather Good Mix of Poems

Alone I wait drinking coffee in back
I have an hour before we start readings
A calm, quiet time to collect, redact
Finish this poem, sort out today's needing's

I hear them now, greeting in the front room
Soon they'll wander on back grabbing a chair
There are maybe fifteen poets, some whom
I know by name, the rest faces seen there

The list is made, I read number five sets
Which is just far enough down to allow
Those here to get ready for my sonnets
I have picked three on love, not that mellow

Polite applause, it's the same for all here
And a rather good mix of poems to cheer

Requires Strength in Purpose

I can still write sonnets with warmth and love
It's a knack I possess, I guard de jure
Of the structure, I find therein much of
The poem resides in ten metered candor

There builds within each of stanza the scope
More so intent of this writer thus said
Perhaps of pros and cons spelled out in hope
That my message is clear, certain and staid

One must be most careful; not be awkward
And lose ones sense of what is then decent
For at this point one needs not go backward
But to advance with this poets intent

To write fourteen lines of verse in meter
Requires strength in purpose and motive sweeter

Resting, My Twinkie

Oh tis sad my son that she is passing
Each has their own moment here on our Earth
Then do honor her with sonnet blessing
That for sixteen years you had her since birth

And such good years they were for I recall
Of trips to far away lands and spaces;
How she would climb upon my lap and sprawl;
Laid–out, jumbled; with joy on our faces

Kept years indoors, I gave her then access
To roam our back, fenced yard; chasing rabbits
Or just resting in the sun; my princess,
She liked RV travel; made these habits

I shall miss her of course for I foresee
Feline Twinkle Toes; resting, my Twinkie

Twinkle Toes was born in September, 1998 and died
at 10 am on Saturday, September 13, 2014. She is buried
along side her brother, Punky Bun and three other cats of ours.

Reveled Till the Sun Rose

Grab your easel and let's go en plein air
I hope that we do then en plein jour pose
Ah, you recall the French we spoke when there
That we drank wine; reveled till the sun rose

Yes, those were years before the War started
You my Alma, young and such a beauty
All the waiters; this way, which way, darted
I would guard you; I felt it my duty

You were gallant Oskar and quite handsome
And we did have moments; oh, I'm sorry
Let us forget youth and enjoy what's come
The day is so special; let's not worry

Alma, all these years I've always loved you
And you Oskar, my heart always was true

Rightly Smitten

Each morn I go to the eastern shoreline
There watch the sun rise fully and brightly
Hoping that its warm rays convey a sign
That you have left Ireland by sail nightly

Each noon I will visit the port entrance
To ask if a lass of reddish tint hair
With lips that match and eyes that flit and glance
Has just arrived with some luggage to bear

Each night I go to mass, there laid my prayer
That safe passage then be given your ship
And fair weather and bright wind lend air
To speed you here safely to lie in slip

Then one day I receive a note written
That you have met someone; rightly smitten

RINGS TRUE THE BELL

Does love break like the boughs off of a tree
When the snow falls wet and binding of weight
And then returns in the spring there to be
Hardy and strong no worse the wear of fight

Does love end with the ships voyage in port
And the fact that it has anchored at shore
In past cruises altered feeling of sort
That now spoils the joy that within you soar

Does my love now suffer from past deeds done
That has no real bearing on our love now
For they were of many years past; not one
Ever rose to shake the plinth of my vow

My love has done much to weather it well
Yet it is strong again, rings true the bell

Rode Off On Horse

I shant trouble you no more M'Lady
And I can show myself the door thank you
With a grand sweep his cape billowed as he
Marched most calmly to the great door, then through

Wait, Lord Duke I implore that you not leave
Perhaps and I say this demurred most plain
Your kind offer I now accept to reave
So please come back, my bed awaits I deign

Amid tea and toast Lord Duke spelled out charade
You will my dear, I now address fondly
Entice the Count to show jewels as played
Then I and masked friend will enter soundly

On the morrow all went as planned of course
And Lord Duke and friend Smythe rode off on horse

ROOM TO BREATHE

I ask myself; do I see you á fond
And my answer is an emphatic; I do
Because I can put me into your pond
Where I swim with those thoughts wondrous of you

And I'm like a youngster watching Callas
Standing in awe of the sound of your voice
Which are vibrant, sending fingers, no less
Up and down my spine; oh that is so nice

I can sense those times when you want distance
We all need these moments; call them hidden
They don't threaten our love; hardly a chance
But they allow us to lose doubt bidden

Oh yes this is a love sonnet I write
To give you room to breathe which is your right

Run–a miss

Thus a fool would refuse a kiss offered
Perhaps, then why a fool is I in doubt
As it comes with strings; thus I have conferred
With none other than my manly Fox scout

He says, and I take him at his word; cease
For to accept the kiss you must promise
Must I promise what; are there palms to grease
No, worse than that; you must marry the Miss

One kiss and I marry; in no way
I would rather kiss a doctor or nurse
She must reach a half–ton; if one could weight
And meals alone would soon bankrupt my purse

Someone else can do this deed for a kiss
Let me off the hook, I'd soon run–a–miss

Says He Knows You

The farm lad came calling, asking for you
Preston told him you weren't at home my dear
Really, I won't have a simple boy who
Because he goes to school with you come here

Mother, his names Matthew, he helps me write
Verse and sonnets that my teacher approves
He's smart in science, topics that give me fright
Please give him the welcome that thus behooves

Emma, I came to your home with a poem
That I hoped would amuse, give you much joy
Matthew I'm so sorry, but I was home
It's just that in this case that you're a boy

Darling, this young man helped me, tis quite true
Doctor Matthew Campbell, says he knows you

SEASON'S CHANGE MOST SUMPTUOUS

Each spring the ducks return to build their nests
And White–Winged Dove fly in to rest and feed
But it is the changing season unrests
Which stirs air and in turn scatters the seed

Each spring my heart restores your love again
Which has lain quite dormant covered with snow
Soon though, frozen blankets will melt; wherein
My parched lips will sip of coolness below

Each spring I long for the bower's bouquet
To waft subtle fragrance from its flowers
Sending my heart then a flutter your way
Wishing you to fill it with love for hours

Each spring I live for your amour, not less
Gotten on the season's change most sumptuous

Secrets I Hold

Tell me now, was the trip up north worthwhile
And did Nordic princess aflame your heart
Tell me the truth for I've not seen you smile
Perhaps you are mourning being apart

I'll not tell of secrets; there were a few
Suffice it that I spent three months in love
Like a water nymph, fresh smelling of dew
She was mentor to my guileless lack of

For she taught me to write as a young child
To make my poems ring of joyful laughter
And to view all nature as God made wild
To see subtle things in divine rapture

Indeed, to her all my secrets were told
So don't ask of me what secrets I hold

Seen Near Trooping

Are you but an erstwhile lover of hers
Among those best gotten to say nothing
For the penance is quite severe for slurs
Of her spoken in foul taverns loathing

Perhaps you'd join with us, become a friend
For we number but two and with you, three
Suggest then our colors are the three tails end
Like those of the mouse, a pattern these be

You ask to what end this trio fights for
Tis well you know for its honor to Queen
That we protect her from those that yell whore
With swords we rise upwards then slice between

Pray not you now confuse this small grouping
With that musket trio seen near trooping

SEND FLOWERS

Words flow rapid when they're spoken of love
Then why writing should cause my pen to slow
Yes I know the structure of poems thereof
Require some thought, but that's something I know

No, it is more complex for as I write
I am thinking of words that have meaning
Ardor, fervor when passion I cite
Intense, perhaps zealous as hearts burning

There is always that fear a word misused
Such as insure your love instead ensure
But that seldom happens if care pursued
In the choosing of words, that you make sure

Well it has now taken nearly two hours
I'd be money ahead to send flowers

Set Our Love Right

You are the light guiding my path onward
And should I then stumble, you're there helping
It's these vital traits that endear comfort
That makes you too special to lose ending

I took love for granted; forgot the hearts
Those same emblems of love that meant so much
Instead, I wrote rambling poems; felt like darts
Straight to your heart; I was clueless, detached

Perhaps too late, but God asks that I try
Simple said; your love means the world to me
We're the perfect pair; have we gone awry
Then let me steer our path to harmony

These past three months have been wondrous delight
So let us once again set our love right

She Now Has an Inkling

It was a most lovely drive to their place
Taking the back road which winds its way there
Farmers were out in fields, John Deere and Case
Even saw a Gleaner and Ford somewhere

Lots of sloughs, no water, there is a drought
And lack of rain has made corn yields pricey
I do wonder if there are fish about
Perhaps in the deep holes they lie dicey

Dick and Jeanie are my family most dear
Outside of our children, none are closer
Slender and tall; me, I'm shorter you hear
He a Marine, I of Navy goes sir

Jeanie and I read poems written last month
She now has an inkling of my nuance

SHIELDS LAKE

When I drove in it was gone; the resort
Bill Grant's place on Shields Lake is a park now
The change complete, no dock, no boats to sort
Even the marsh Cattails missing somehow

There was a time after the big world war
When Mom and Dad took us to Bill Grant's place
For a couple of weeks Dad served Grant's bar
And we then stayed at his house; leisured pace

From our southern State came farmers fishing
Cane poles with hooked worms they fished for Bullheads
In flat bottom, wooden boats; all day thing
They'd take their lunch, some beer, maybe some meds

While this went on all of summer we played
Caught small Tadpoles, made sure the boats belayed

Should I Go Back to Bed

I felt that nudge; are you waking darling
I hear not an answer; must be asleep
Just a dream in action; was it parling
Again the nudge; closer with love you creep

And then you have me, my arms are pinned down
And warm kisses keep me busy; oh see
I'm now awake in more ways than one shown
You lift your face and say; morning honey

I must counter–attack, so I tickle
And roll over, my strength favored as male
Giggling you sprawl and say don't be fickle
Come love me, make my day joyous and hale

Now I wonder should I go back to bed
Or will that keep me from being then fed

SHOULD I THEN STAY

It is true love; nothing else it could be
For my heart beats only for one so dear
Do not doubt me Thomas, surely you'll see
That fresh sparkle in her manner appear

There is a bounce as she comes now running
Then leaps to press herself so close; and then
All the warmth of summer; oh so cunning
Is she as my passion stirs now within

Please God let this wondrous feeling linger
To give calor to my hungry ardor
Such heat inflames me as I now finger
Her hair softly with such gentile candor

I love how she begins my day this way
With the promise of more should I then stay

Signaled by a Sennet

Oh fair moon, you shining orb of romance
Beam your rapture unto my arms this night
So that I may enfold her and enhance
Nay, much more; heighten my love in her sight

I see you now peeking oe'r the mountain
Are you spying on me; making then sure
That I am here alone in my kitchen
Then shame on you as my motives are pure

But now you have risen; oh my Luna
Can you forgive me; that I would asperse
Yet not seen in glory had I sooner
Viewed such august of sight ne'er wouldst coerce

Then I pray thee grant this lame brained poet
His wish for love signaled by a sennet

Sennet: a signal call on a trumpet

Silly Bike Stunts We Did

I've gone and done it, bought myself a bike
Twenty–six inch wheels with knobby road tires
Bright red and I have a helmet matched like
Sits on soda can made alloy and wires

The name Mongoose, agile Cobra hunter
But will have to accept Rattlers instead
My trial runs on asphalt, old man wonder
Won't try any jumps, that's not for me I've read

My friend Bruce, now there's a real bike rider
He bikes miles in double digits for fun
A real touring; could be racing idler
I'm not in his league but I'll make the run

Some will say I just want to be a kid
Recall all those silly bike stunts we did

SIMPLE PLEASURES

Simple pleasures; what does their lack portend
Is my life so complex, is that then why
I can't sample leisure, nor to pretend
When I dream of boyhood, of thoughts gone by

There's this theory that now badgers my mind
That I am so engaged in poems I write
That I haven't the time, nor have opined
Why this act of pursuit I would invite

I then persist that I'm driven in this
That I have stored away thoughts so profound
My times passing quickly, this I witness
As it confirms this wish of mine resound

Then it is blessed; by whom, does it matter
And no simple pleasures I take gather

Simple What Comes Around

Softness becomes my bed, spacious and wide
I'll then reside on the left side tonight
Always the side further from bath confide
In time I will reverse, bed on the right

I've laid sort of mishmash of sheets homespun
There are plenty of sets; bedding I have
But none flannel as I prefer that one
Is that a quirk, perhaps as that's my fave

I will redo the spare bedroom in pink
For when Maiah comes here she'll like the room
A place for women, not men I think
They would rather it be liken a tomb

There now, already I am cheered and feel fine
Simple what comes around taken the time

SIMPLY LOSS OF FOCUS

There I've done it, made things complex again
Fiddled with your mindset, confused measures
I should have left these thoughts alone just then
And stayed the course and not opened fissures

But I worry about my love taut mêne
Is it fragile for I know not your pain
You have my poems, certain you have read them
But all I have are your paintings as lain

I feel we have bonded; my heart's speaking
Yet I could be pushing too hard; maybe
Oh tis of such misery, my poems breaking
The limbs of trees as I rush on towards thee

Has my long drive deranged my thought process
And these last poems simply loss of focus

SIR WILLIAM WALLACE

Scottish hero, this Sir William Wallace
His life spanning thirty–five years only
A true common peasant without much grace
But a leader of worth would soon rally

At the battle near the Stirling Castle
Wallace forced the English from North Scotland
He met fifty thousand soldiers by rill
And on the bridge ambush those from England

Wallace then lost at the Falkirk battle
And forced into retreat; then was captured
And in London Tower felt death's rattle
Never to see Scotland's freedom furthered

Ten years after his death Scotland was free
Robert the Bruce would reign; Wallace ne'er be

Six Bits

Mister; how much for that book of sonnets
You mean the one covered with dust right there
Yes; but I have only about six bits
Would you sell it even if it's quite rare

Six bits; hmmm; that's about seventy–five cents
A sum mighty, one might then say if asked
And that book is priceless the bard laments
But tell me Miss why this purchase is tasked

I have heard of sonnets written most bold
That speak of love that the poet wrote here
That it perdure for an entŕ acte; I'm told
Yet it resumed in their seventy–fifth year

I'll sell as asked but tell me how you know
You see Sir, I knew them both long ago

Sleep is Most Helpful

Comes now my time; careful must I then be
For these are hearts fragile and age most cruel
No more would youth shake–off as if a flea
Rather than hurt by least profound the rule

I could of course take no action opting
Which my Elf says is the simple answer
So why make a Mole hill out of nothing
When just keeping quiet makes peace ensure

I shall sleep on this now; awake then fresh
And find indeed that there is no problem
Perhaps with dreams I'll hear my voice say hush
Sleep then gentile, repose and make with REM

I am told that this sleep is most helpful
If so then I could use a week then full

So Count Yourself Lucky

Often love comes like a warmed up gusher
Playing on one's body, prickling of heat
Little the drops that seep and give pleasure
Heralds romance with its advent replete

When this happens, the world is your oyster
You'll fly with Blue Angels, dive with Cousteau
Eat at the best restaurants, dance with Astaire
Fall then asleep like there is no morrow

Dizzy or just giddy; spinning all day
Is it the flu bug or have you a cold
You try then to shake it, send it away
But it's in your bloodstream, gotten a hold

So count yourself lucky when love comes round
As these things do happen lately I've found

So He Writes of Truth

When I speak with fervor do you listen
For I would come in an instant to you
When I cry with the Wolves do you beckon
Even if it meant I'd trek by snowshoe

What then drives this poet to such actions
And thus writes such lucid poems and sonnets
Could it be my knowledge rivals doyens
That I'll herald the smell of fresh vi'lets

Or do I have special powers hidden
To see future; foreknow what will happen
And then allow me to do what's bidden
As does Sherlock Holmes and sidekick Watson

When a poet's in love his minds active
So he writes of truth or is it fictive

So Much Could be Written

Such is my joy; I have gotten your note
For it came just this morn dappled with hearts
I blushed red in hue when read what you wrote
Then read and re–read it over of parts

The phrase where I'm likened to a Rosebud
That waits for the moment when you draw near
To burst into flower, nascent your nod
Then picked for your pleasure, holding sincere

At night when it's quiet, no one's about
Read then by moon light the part I loved best
Holding me for ever, never in doubt
Telling of those kisses you have confessed

When notes and fond letters brought love in prose
So much could be written left to suppose

Some Form of Trap

She came marching right by me in two–stepped
Didn't seem to see me; she passed on by
What was on her mind; that she then well kept
A gal of some secrets, but not a spy

I'll not wonder if she even comes back
I'm not the sole flower in her bower
As a matter–of–fact I'm just a hack
Beneath her feet; I couldn't then be lower

Still, I always wished she'd give me a glance
To say just my name would raise up my hope
So much that I then might ask her to dance
But that's not in the cards; she'd just say nope

I will have to devise some form of trap
But then she'd call for the cops; help, kidnap

Some May Say His Intent

It's his hand print, that's how he signs his name
You mean that's all, no strange symbols either
Well there is that mark he makes; now don't blame
My art gallery; we just hang his works here

Look at this Mir; see if I hold my hand
Against the stone and then blow this mixture
Oh, it's magic Gothar; your hand is grand
Now I will know your hand marks your picture

Well I think it is quite striking; his sign
You can even see the whorls and loops there
His own fingers; and his prints I would deign
Hard to copy that; I wonder now where...

These cave drawings; you see the hand imprint
Marks the artist; some may say his intent

Someone Complain of Riot

Does the city have an ordinance on noise
If so then they should quell the loud ruckus
Rock bands playing somewhere with not much poise
It's now going on towards midnight or plus

I then gather this is special tonight
Perhaps a fete; some kind of grand concert
I now wonder what the neighbors make light
Of, this assault on my quiet desert

I am getting tired so maybe I'll sleep
And if I keep music of my CD's
At a higher level, the beat won't seep
Through my bedroom walls, I will rest ease

This is all quite irksome; I like quiet
Why then doesn't someone complain of riot

Sonnets I've Penned

Why must these sad memories persist in thought
The time is long past and I must forget
And not think they too are feeling distraught
For it is my quagmire that I have let

Is it fancy of me; as a poet
I would reply I need to feel these things
To write of love I must also know it
And that entails the pains of heart breakings

And what could top that of firsthand knowledge
Like a seasoned warrior knows of defeat
And can rejoice as a victor might judge
I too will soar with love knownst to entreat

Perhaps then my memories are a godsend
Which I can draw on in sonnets I've penned

Sonnets That Speak of Love

Who speaks of words transformed thus to my ear
That I gather to lay as poems intact
Fashioned of love's lambent romance and tears
Do I have then recourse of harm in fact

Or am I the arrow shot by archer
Wending its way, merely guileless in name
A pawn no less of my minds own capture
Then be this so I must accept the blame

For I am but poet, no more no less
Spinner of tales and love affairs in rhyme
Meant to gladden ones heart in joy and bliss
And if perchance of rue then salve of thyme

Then let me write poems of verse, thus avers
Sonnets that speak of love that soon conquers

Stands Me Well in Stature

I have tried poems of a different nature
But I write less of verse without rhyming
As so many do with éclat I'm sure
That my absence even of prose, nothing

For my notice is in sonnets I write
Of love, romance, even of tales once told
Perhaps venture of verse as to incite
In my readers more of mystique of old

Ah, but of love I choose to write sonnets
In the style of Shakespeare; he's my master
So I plead to forgive my use of its
Style, so olde of England's words and grammar

Let me then pen my poems most of structure
As rhymed meter stands me well in stature

STILL, I HEAR THEM IN MY HEART

So much was never said; put–off, forgot
But that is gone, destroyed over aeons
Those stilled voices once heard within earshot
Did they soothe the aching heart with paeans

A most thun'drus singing tone he possessed
To be able to stand at the edge there
With the ocean waves then crashing with zest
And thrill within hearing his songs premiere

Oh he was an imposing figure this man
Straight forward his eyes; did he see us
Were his visions then true as they began
That in millions of years one would discuss

I will never know those voices long gone
Still, I hear them in my heart then anon

STROLLING THE BEACH

Let's go shelling, looking for those pretties
Walking the beach bare feet digging; there's one
The shells plenty washed up by wave eddies
But these are dull, their shell luster now gone

But if you soak them in water they change
And some with a rub of baby oil made
Heightens faded color, so then arrange
In a glass vial; recall the fun you played

Now if you want live shells you need get wet
Snorkel the reefs, turn the rocks; SCUBA
I've done all these, even dredged the deep, yet
I'd soon treasure a beach shell of Cuba

It's not the sea shell that matters that much
It is strolling the beach, keeping in touch

Strong Women

I have always believed in strong women
Strong in the sense of some moral duty
Whether in the speaking of wrongs by men
Or of seeking justice for its beauty

I find myself baffled thereof men's wrongs
Why then under supposed aegis of them
Has it perdured, was this sanctioned aeons
For it still is extant this day a' men

Now take justice; some are therefore winners
And the losers, how best succor, appease
In a perfect world there are no sinners
So this won't be timely, hardly of ease

I'll not herald the giant strides that were made
Until the male cogent world is allayed

SULLEN PITY

From where do I return my mind betwixt
I have this drive, it has bothered aeons
At least a half century taken its licks
Like a millstone remained fixed now beyond

Oh what's this taste, this lump within my soul
Should cause such pain, such joy to mix conjoined
Ne'er then it be resolved, some salve as toll
Which I'd gladly pay in full once then coined

Alas, tis a windmill that I joust now
And it will soon unseat me de facto
Leaving my trip home of disgrace I bow
Yet still telling of my conquests back too

I've asked myself what I would make of thee
To change this sad story, sullen pity

Tacit and Clear

I see you have gotten a blue berry
Instead of bran muffin; why the change yet
Ah, I see it in your eyes, how merry
And your smile, you have now a big secret

Cannot I hide my joy; is it patent
And spread throughout my face saying its love
I'll not deny tis true but my intent
Was not to flaunt, as in your face to shove

No, no it's more subtle, but I detect
Even those moods slightly given by you
Your face is an open book; now don't object
Cats know much more than the common folks do

Is it no small wonder why I come here
For my poet's mind is tacit and clear

TALKING WITH MASTER WILL

I sat last night talking with Master Will
And the topics ran from war onto love
He was surprised that his plays did so well
A rich man he would certain to be guv

When I mentioned I wrote sonnets, he asked
If I believed in the form; I said yes
And he was pleased, I could tell; so I basked
In his warm reception; most pleasing this

I told him about the movie I'd seen
Shakespeare In Love and the plot in few words
His laughter I believe hid the ravine
That deepened and he said a few swearwords

I bid him goodbye; no mention was made
Of further parlance, and the bill; unpaid

Target Fixate

When a shipmate was lost we all felt numb
Trying hard to stay on track of our jobs
But that passed by quickly, mourning was dumb
All it got you was to thinking and sobs

No, we'd leave that later for drinks of draft
I can recall a flight into Laos
Twas two sections of our squadron aircraft
Again quite dark with no lights to guide us

As I pulled g's after releasing my own
I saw a flash to south of my posit
Then the call from section two; one plane down
As the fireball vanished; a friend bought it

After landing our talks about focus
Target fixate; so POW bogus

Tear Stained of Pain

Each night as I lay half asleep dreaming
Hoping to see your face appear to me
I shall wait through night's fall as if seeming
Any minute to cry, it's you I see

Oh what torture I feel as I love you
Must you coquette with all strangers nearby
For it tears my heart so; you then tease too
As if I could return witty reply

Must I then be cuckold, all friends to see
For I will hate you; dare I say gladly
Why you do this to me; pray have mercy
Spare this life I would now end so sadly

Each morn upon waking the same again
My bed tussled and torn, tear stained of pain

Telling Such a Whopper

Catch the wind and then be lifted onward
To sail high with twirling eddies of air
I meet the most piquant of things brought toward
My path; why just minutes ago a hare

But I digress for my journey resumes
And soon I'm joined by loud, honking ganders
Who ask me point–blank who sells the best plumes
For they are now wearing pairs of panniers

Is that why those saddle bags you carry
Well then you don't expect to trail feathers
Like a kite's tail; no sir, these bags we ferry
Exact a fair penny too for tethers

I hear my wife calling time for supper
She'll scold me too; telling such a whopper

THAT HE LOVES ME

It will be hard leaving you this Sunday
God makes these trials, testing then our resolve
For he knows that winners rejoice one day
And the losers pray God one day absolves

Tis best you know to keep yourself busy
And with grandkids you won't have that problem
I of course shall head south to my poe'sy
Where my composure is not of aplomb

We will survive; think of Inga and Thor
And the thousands like them leaving Norway
While their mailings were slow; emails du jour
And cellphone calls will salve the sting away

I can offer four words; that I love you
Then your mantra; that he loves me, rings true

THAT I AM WHAT I AM

We have come a long way in these short weeks
Sharing my poems and your paintings en masse
These are what the poet in my soul seeks
What fuels my vast genius of poems amass

But have I been selfish scoring of love
For you may be pensive, wary perhaps
Of what this man's after, what's he made of
Be it honor and not that of mishaps

Let time be the manner for which I'm judged
Give me a year, I could hardly ask more
And I will show wisdom, none of it fudged
As our dealings of love evens the score

I give you this pledge, hold dear within
That I am what I am; honest therein

That I Feel No Remorse

There was no call, nothing to show she'd left
And I suppose I knew all that before
Still I had hoped; who wants to feel bereft
'Specially when we enjoyed such great rapport

Oh I knew all about the cruise she'd take
I was at the Christmas party last year
When white slippers were gifts; but none I'd stake
This was family; I was simply veneer

And since her son had made this gift to her
There would be seven; and me, I quoth
Wasn't even thought of; I'm the chauffeur
Asked to come north to drive her back and forth

I will take my own cruise; by land of course
And pray to god that I feel no remorse

THAT I HAVE NOW CHOSEN YOU

She comes in stealth mode this feline of mime
Then hops upon my bed; finds her safe lie
And when convinced, curls up for it is time
And she hasn't said one meow or cry

I know she is thinking about you Anne
For she listens to our cell phone calls too
And then sometimes I can detect again
That smile almost human as if she knew

Will she miss me; will I miss her; God knows
But I couldn't drag her with me; oh no
She's not ready to move; put though the throws
Of car trips; strange places to sleep; all that woe

We make choices all our lives; this isn't new
That I have now chosen you; this she knew

THAT I PROPOSE TO LAY

Going home now that I'm alone, I sigh
Wouldst I have done this had not death happen
And the answer came out, no way wouldst I
You too Bruce, might well have traveled spoken

No, we both have our lives on a new path
And I'm trying very hard to grasp gist
As there has to be some nous that's not wrath
Could that be to writing my poems insist

Then let me sit looking over the town
To write of sights we saw long, long ago
That will append our brief space and time shown
As a gentle sojourn in life's garden we sow

I'm not at this moment able to say
The deep meaning that I propose to lay

THAT I'M SURE OF

I knew you were special when we first met
As it is a poet's talent possessed
To be able to see this as tacit;
Then when I'm all alone, write poems with zest

It's that Elfish glimmer in your right eye
And the way you smile that causes my heart
To beat like a tom–tom that's gone awry,
And cause longed for kisses when we're apart

The most simple of joys; to see you here
To be greeted with an embrace and kiss,
Then feel your strong power that you share dear
As this means that my day's full of bliss

I am firm of belief that in time; love
Comes to every person; that I'm sure of

That it Becomes Our Home

I seek open prairie and no mountains
Land that's fertile with game; pray all survive
I want to see parks with flowing fountains
And places friendly; spoken English implied

I want to see the sun rise in the east
The warm glow seen briefly as it becomes
It's whole self to spread warmth to man and beast
And high above give life to Roses and Mums

Then in the late of day when the sun dips
And the sky turns purple and pink–red hues
I shall get my fill of life in small sips
And then content, lay still my head with dews

I take this land to share with you in love
That it becomes our home I pledge thereof

THAT IT COULD THEN HAPPEN

Why can't life be just a simple matter
With give and take and no questions beseeched
Is it because we must always splatter
The ones we love with muck; thus we've been teached

Then I propose that we ponder this bid
That a day of each week be laid aside
To patch up the wrongs no matter who did
Then start afresh, each to promise; abide

Now on a scale larger, include the world
Just think, no new fighting; this could catch on
And soon order would be restored; unfurled
The flags of peace as strife would then begone

The best of times; this make believe drama
That it could then happen; become karma

THAT JUST HIT RUSSIA

I went out last night to view shooting stars
That flashed across, likened streaks of white paint
Only to meet their death, as in Star Wars
And yet frequent a piece survives that's quaint

They call those that survive a name different
For this rock chunk (I use that term lightly)
Could have brought life early; instead, thus spent
Its thrust in a display case of glassie

Some nights are more active; I just wonder
Are there pockets of meteors that race
Suppose it is random, as when yonder
Clusters of stars lose their loads to vast space

I'm glad these pieces burn up before crashing
Like the one that just hit Russia, smashing

That My Poems Speak Wonders

Oh just write on you bard of no concern
As if there was anyone that might listen
To your poems of love; of what would they learn
How to measure meter or rhyme kissin'

Now hold on here fair Muse; careful you poke
As a flood of rapture, squirting may sway
Your view cockeyed; are all critics now broke
So you have to write this claptrap for pay

I am told by one whose knowledge sublime
That my sonnets thrill her; wouldst she thus lie
I'd tell you her name but really no time
As I'm due at Black Cat Sunday's poem fry

If you want a label then use unique
That my poems speak wonders unknownst to weak

THAT PLAYS TO CROWDS

You're my vanguard, all hope rest there upon
And should a foe intrude, not of welcome
You wouldst gladly lay your life down as done
Such then wouldst my grateful largesse become

But what folly has put me now at risk
That I need, nay require this force in arms
I have no horde of old bullion or disk
That wouldst warrant a home attack of harms

Perhaps they seek my poems that aren't published
Or could it be that they only want me
That I have now stumbled upon what's wished
By these kidnap crooks that threaten maybe

Such these ramblings of an erstwhile poet
That plays to crowds for their tendresse knows it

THAT SHOULD APPEAR CONDIGN

What do you see; has a feline passed by
You sit heedful for now what's caught your eye
Perhaps it is nothing, a bird flown high
A mere shadow just caste across the sky

I must marvel at your patience my friend
To sit so still, ne'er twitch your tail at all
And so trance–like, enthralled what chance did send
For I've watched you calmly there by the wall

Do you miss her; you know of whom I speak
Does she send you signal you view alone
I would never doubt this message you seek
As I too have received words of atone

Tell me, wouldst you confide to me what's seen
Yes, I expect that should appear condign

That You'd Roll a Seven

My mind is a twixt to call her cell phone
For it has been almost two weeks of none
Yet I say to myself, why not postpone
These urges I have and let silence just run

If I could just call her as a dear friend
Ask her advice; wouldst her answers truthful
For how could we both cleave what our hearts send
No, it is a fool's wish of those youthful

Yet I sit here wond'ring; does she pine too
And does her heart flutter, ending with sigh
As this is what I feel; and yet, adieu
These fond ardors; tis most folly belie

Will St. Peter say when ent'ring heaven
Were you afraid that you'd roll a seven

THAT'S WHY I LOVE YOU

If I were to cease this very instant
And fly off to heaven, then no greater
Love would I find than what now of intent
Has blessed my heart; thus I'd die in rapture

If I were to seek love without warning
And have every wish of ardent feeling
It still wouldn't match the kiss this morning
That you gave me; my brain still then reeling

If I were to hear the music just made
By a band of angels; the sound then heard
Would soon pale when compared to your parade
Blaring trumpets and loud drummers when neared

To me you best every similar event
That's why I love you with fervent advent

THE CAT LOOKED OUT WITH GLEE

Falls a coming shouted the Grey Squirrel
I felt it this morning gath'ring my nuts
You must hurry; snow will come till April
Drifting to great depths; my tree it abuts

You're so active drawled the fattened Woodchuck
Me, I'd rather lie here in the sunshine
While you, Squirrel are now running amok
I, in my hole, listen to the wind whine

Quit your squeaking said the Goose at the lake
When the snow flies I'll be heading southwards
To bask in the warm gulf flats to partake
Of choice shoots and leaves of grass and Collards

Watching from the window, warm as can be
Smiling a bit, the Cat looked out with glee

The Coffee Shop

Where have all my storefronts now gone away
I look out The Coffee Shop's front windows
And they glare back, hawking new names they say
Subway, The Cheese Cave and Piercing Tattoo's

Faintly I hear crying; here Jim and Joes
Next to Kresge's; you know the dime store place
And down the way, Duncan's Photo to pose
Don't you forget me too Hurry Back space

Even this place I sit drinking coffee
Was a pool hall, blue with cigar smoke haze
Forgot what the name was; dark place to be
With its table of felt, steely eyes gaze

Now the cycle riders, tall and slim come
Grab their lattes, take sips, they're on the run

The Crowd Cheering

As luck might have it, I happened upon
A bright shiny object there on the ground
And when diving to see it; poof it's gone
Leaving a red stain; oh surely a wound

Wond'ring; I climbed, my mind all a flutter
For what reason would a wizard cast spells
That would entice me to notice clutter
Being a stunt pilot doing chandelles

But then I did recall my arch rival
Wanting me to crash; he'd use sleight of hand
And of course my Elf; who wouldn't snivel
Made sure of my air show for the grandstand

Tis a wondrous life; this being of flight
The crowd cheering as I'm in the limelight

The Deep Vault of Daydreams

There are times when romance is at my door
And I feel of rapture surging within
Then do fill my lonely heart with amour
And in concert lifting my thoughts therein

Had I not been listening to songs idyll
Wouldst I not then scrieve my pen with fondness
And write sweet words of love that is until
The mood changing, that of sorrow's loneness

I tell my heart there is room there for all
And I wouldst then gladly take all in fold
Alas I have not the means for this call
So I shall keep instead these thoughts untold

Look then into the deep vault of daydreams
For there within this poem appears and gleams

THE DOGS WON'T AGGRESS

Deep in winter's slumber we lay about
A time to spend indoors, warm and toasty
And I with my notepad, pen and Wite–Out
Have just settled in; all comfy roasty

There's a light snow dusting; blown with the breeze
Like ash from a fire storm falls to the ground
I need not then bother blizzards to ease
For all is quite tranquil; coldness abound

Heavens I have just now wakened from sleep
Did I doze long; my poem wasn't finished
These cat naps are wondrous and not a peep
Dogs made in my cellar; silence I'd wished

Sometimes after dosing my mind's a mess
Till I recall that the dogs won't aggress

THE GIRLS OF ST. MARY'S

I see the steps where long ago we sat
Bundled up with caps smug, it was winter
Were we two and three years, perhaps at that
For we'd visit Grandma's house to enter

Grandpa Ole wearing a suit; quiet
It may have been Sunday, thus our picture
I can't recall his voice, it was nigh yet
Nineteen thirty–nine and not a fixture

Had my dad grown up here by St. Mary's
The play field fenced to shield young girls playing
Was their romance, covert of course, stories
Would be told, a call made, no more saying

In high school both Dick and I were dating
The girls of St. Mary's, love gone waiting

THE HEARTS OF NATURE

The scent of my flowers reminds of spring
Essence of sweet fragrance floats to my nose
And I inhale with deep gulps; ah to wring
Out all of the perfume of the primrose

It's the honey–suckle that now captures
And I'm tipsy and quite mellow; could be
I'm drunk as my head is swirling, raptures
Leave me dizzy so I grab for a tree

Then when settling down in soft and lush grass
My head resting, cozy in moss now new
I am thinking; what can ever surpass
This fine moment laced with sundew

My thoughts turn to Karen when in this mood
When I sense the hearts of nature exude

THE KEY THAT UNLOCKS

When all else fails a sonnet warms her heart
And you wonder; does she think of me now
Specially when she has left you; gone apart
Does a tear stain her bodice of sorrow

Tell her of the love that wells up within
That if you hear not from her you will die
Your heart that will surely burst forth sanguine
A thousand deaths until her breast you lie

But a sonnet must give forth hope as well
To be at her beck and command always
And to that end you pledge love without fail
As in the fall the last yellow Rose stays

Oh true love is fraught with many roadblocks
Yet to her heart you've the key that unlocks

THE LAYMAN AFAR

Sitting around, the four of us appeased
Never a more kindred group was seen here
I would listen of such rapture they seized
Sprinkled with soft jabs; bon vivant their fare

Who brought up the seniors dot com web site
Perhaps it slipped out, a faux pas misspoke
But then questions arose; really did bite
With a sigh of relief it passed as joke

But I digress as our concern not tales
No, we sampled of Peach pie a la mode
So good I waived concerns of weight gain wails
And would stifle desire; another piece bode

I feel honored as the layman afar
Sanctioned as one of the circle as par

The Pains of Search and Stress

Somewhere there is love and I will find it
Thought I search the world in every corner
It still eludes me; it remains secret
Am I destined then a life as loner

That I refuse outright for I'm stubborn
And will perdure in this quest to find her
For she exists; oh yes, this one was born
And lives some place waiting for me ever

When this moment happens such joy my heart
And to hold her tightly telling of love
As I have found the one, never to part
Our lives conjoined there now that I'm sure of

Grant this wish to foretell of love's mistress
That saves me from the pains of search and stress

THE PASSIONS OF YOUTH IN LOVE

You went away and left me there alone
Had this caught me surprised, perhaps you too
For had I known wouldst then I make atone
But no matter for it's done, that I rue

Was it then fate...oh how I hate that word
Surely I could have changed my life around
Had you given a sign, steered me onward
Instead I was left to fail and I drowned

And now I yearn fifty–five years later
To hear a word spoken; it is forgive
But that will not happen; makes no matter
For my feelings of no concern; I'll live

Complex is the passions of youth in love
Yet it is the simplest to stand clear of

The Pre-flight

My plane captain meets me; it's my pre–flight
We exchange glances; it's too noisy for talk
He's taken my helmet and that's alright
I duck under the wing; it's a cake–walk

Check cap fastened on center–line fuel tank
Tonight's load; Mark eighty two and three bombs
That's fifteen hundred pounds each wing to yank
Making sure they're on tight; I've got no qualms

I finish my walk–around and then pause
I'll check the gross weight; heavy load tonight
The ladder held, I climb as the ship yaws
We're turning to wind; I'm ready to light

The jet engine screams, its power now felt
I'm snug in my cockpit; what war has dealt

THE QUEEN WON'T MIND

My love, she goes in frills; gathered in pleats
About her neck and on her wrists about
And black stockings, there so dainty now meets
Black shoes, buckled which gleam, going then out

At last she waves and mouths sly goodbye
Then like a grey Rabbit scampers away
Leaving a plume of her essence on nigh
I am giddy; my smile widens they say

Lord Duke, Lord Duke; wake up the Queen is here
I must have just fallen asleep; fiddles
Show the Lady to my quarters my dear
Then tell the chef, two for dinner; vittles

I must resume that dream after dinner
The Queen won't mind, she knows that I'm a sinner

THE RIGHT BUTTONS PUSHED IN LOVE

This is a great pleasure we have achieved
And it has now converged to this instance
For we've come full circle and not deceived
Nor have we been slackened by the distance

That this is true friendship we will declare
And don't forget the love that binds us strong
And there's kindness in what manners we share
As we strive to do what's righteous; not wrong

Oh, there are few different postures we view
The way we see the world; tis Rose or Blue
Or if we both believe in God; we do
For our friendship needs that anchor; tis true

We have achieved what's called reason thereof
When all the right buttons are pushed in love

The Tumbling of Rills

How do I write a trill; a warble flutter
This has been my question ever since when
To make my lines of rhymed meter utter
In words that then flutter; excite within

To trill or not to trill depends on skill
And few can then master this with much ease
But two; Lily Pons and Jennie Tourel
Were so perfect; always the crowd to please

But a bird can warble; they will say so
And I have heard early springtime singing
A most pleasing sound through open window
Cheerful warbles; they're mating calls then ringing

Oh such pleasure to hear warbles and trills
Rapture I feel, like the tumbling of rills

THEIR FORT ASSAILED

Chinese year two thousand fourteen is named
The year of the horse that is made of wood
Not a special time as western's acclaimed
Unless one then reverts back to childhood

Then a wooden horse brings back good memories
When you rode at gallop, chased by some thieves
Your steed frothing, panting welcomes the breeze
You loose then an arrow as your horse weaves

Quick to the fort; mother has called supper
Those wild robbers will just have to tarry
Steak and mushrooms, the meal will be super
Then back to the action; swords to parry

I will caution as a wooden horse failed
Those men of Troy were duped; their fort assailed

THEN ALSO BE DELUSIVE

My love has flown far, far away to stay
In the country that's called Costa Rica
Where exactly I cannot, will not say
But I thank God it's not Tanganyika

There will be no cell phone calls she has said
And emails and text messages also
A lonely week for me; probably sad
My mood as I try to forget, ergo

But a week's not forever I've been told
Although my heart is not convinced of that
Still I have survived greater lengths ninefold
And in a week we'll be back for chit–chat

I'm grasping at straws as love's illusive
For it might then also be delusive

Then Please Explain My Poems

I might throw a dart at Ireland's map guides
Say ten feet from so as not to pick spot
And when the map is pierced, a town decides
To be my base, locus of points estop

Bed and Breakfast with few people drawn near
By a lake or marshy canal I'll park
To write sonnets of love's devotion so dear
And tales of past kings and their wars I mark

I am intrigued by the Shannon's Lough Ree
It is central and could well be darts end
I've now seen the Elfins, Ardagh they be
What sure magic draws me towards this spot friend

Say I'm merely dreaming, that this comes naught
Then please explain my poems Ireland has wrought

There Can Be No Greater Love

Planning our life as we gather insights
Into of each other's journeys that made
Us more conscious of love, honor and rights
Has now given us a sense of what's laid

We feel sanguine with each other to trust
Our lives and those values held close to heart
We know that there could be bathos; yet just
As well we will harvest love from the start

For I am thus honest in my love here
And wouldst it be latent, then let it pour
Forth in gushing élan so all can hear
Of this joyous rapture held dear therefore

Let me speak most clearly, for of love known
There can be no greater love than I've shown

THERE NO GREATER LOVE WROTE

The words; "Think of me" from "The Phantom..." sang
By Christine and Raoul seem so fitting
As you mentioned tonight, for we both rang
So you were thinking of me; remitting

And I of course think of you constantly
When I drink my morning coffee you're there
And when I drive to town I glance gently
Hoping to see your smile, my Solitaire

When I write my poems I must concentrate
For I tend to write love poems, Anne–Marit
You are my focus, the reason I wait
When I think of you my poems stand apart

In years to come when my sonnets are read
There no greater love wrote it will be said

They Are All For You

Oh my sweet I'm a poor one to explain
How my mind works, much less my poetry
But ye must know never could I chicane
I write poems; my life not of coquetry

So I write of heartbreak, of love destroyed
As I write of happiness and love give'n
For the moods of readers, whether cowboy'd
Or ploughboy'd depends how their life be rive'n

Then many of my poems are not of love
They are an eclectic array of themes
Not having a thing to do with hereof,
Whereof or thereof, but only of dreams

I hope this makes sense; they are all for you
But how you interpret each I eschew

They Ply Me with Notions

Often I've dreamt of those elfin friends dear
That keeps constant their watch over just me
And if you ask plainly, I'll tell sincere
That what I dream is not public you see

There's a special branch of Elves for poets
Long and hard they labor much like recruits
Skilled in love trysts, readers of poems; misfits
Picked for hidden talents and strange salutes

Once they've chosen you, best you not deny
As their antics might well keep you busy
And then no poems you'll write so don't belie
Them or give them cause as they'll act hussy

As for myself I find no faults this time
They ply me with notions, my own goldmine

They'll Now Pester Me to Play

I write the night and the night writes of us
And on my bed compose these thoughts now true
That I can do this each night startles thus
But I perdure of task; render to you

Many the nights I have sat here stagnant
My mind bemused with thoughts random, disjoint
Until in a moment sparks fly rampant
And words flow then easy to my pen point

For the nights my Phoenix; time to rev up
Get those juices flowing, finish my poem
And then I can relax take time to sup
Read a book and listen to songs of home

Tis a full moon tonight and Sprites come out
They'll now pester me to play, run about

They'll Want Me to Cease

Sitting here way above Central, my view
Of the paved street below, I watch the cars
Driving back and forth, in front seats they're two
It's called dragging Central, too young for bars

It is Friday night, a movie showing downtown
At the Village where the bathrooms aren't gross
Like the other where back rows hush each moan
And young couples in love tumble and toss

After the show, maybe fries and a coke
Listen to the jukebox, there's Blue Suede Shoes
But its only noise as chatters invoke
Cupped ears, there is gossip, whispers, you knows

Suppose I should get down before police
See me up here cause they'll want me to cease

THINK OF ME AS BROTHER

Have I hurt you; I meant no harm or pain
You know of me, my life is thus open
And though I've penned sonnets you see now lain
My poems reek of false love, promises broken

But that is what poets do; lay sorrow
In their footsteps, then they scurry to fix
Playing some vice against what they borrow
Tis far better to stand distant, not mix

What then is my worth that you would welcome
I am loyal, perhaps not in love, but
Steadfast a friend for life and not one rum
But most honest and quite stalwart of cut

Maybe you should think of me as brother
That way romance in my poems won't bother

This Makes Me Feel Happy

I am content to sit waiting at home
Reading a book; writing a poem, I might
Perhaps even view a movie on Rome
Or just listen to my CDs at night

But if you were present the mood alters
We'd have dinner for two; candles lit too
I'd wash dishes, fill peppers and salters
Then a coffee; mine strong, decaf for you

There would be time for some quiet moments
When we could just relax and do métier
You to painting and I penning sonnets
The rest of the evening we might just play

Sharing our loves; having you here all days
This makes me feel happy; in love always

This May Be Kismet

Do not fault me for I love you dearly
Tis a reason that we sunder a spell
There are some souls within this small city
That don't condone affairs; that's a pity

It would be more prudent for you to own
Of a separate pied-à-tere alone
Of course to rent would then suffice as well
Then our courtship resumes; we're free to mell

Myself, I do favor renting a place
But then there's the need to sell your home base
And when we do wed, as surely we will
We won't need two homes as one fits the bill

This is the best of worlds so don't forget
Our love is stronger, this may be kismet

This Night's Delight

What was the poem about, you seemed amorous
Oh it was love indeed, shall I read it
Yes please do, I marvel your poems sensuous
But come to bed and read what you have writ

That's all I've written, so kiss me sweet
And from this fond embrace let stars sparkle
Within your eyes, let the moon then compete
With my ardor as these pleasures instill

Let me trace with fingers these paths I take
To taste the fruit dulcet and much honeyed
And hear sounds made softly that you can make
As we drift off into slumber wide eyed

I love your poem's ending, be sure to write
It down in the morning, this night's delight

THIS ONE I WOULD HOLD

It is a hand lying gently alone
For it rests on no form, unless I'd guess
It is a shape human, but sees no bone
Or clear feature, is it a shroud, then yes

Perhaps I have this wrong, the hand is key
And all comments should address that fact
For I see they're caring, sorrow, maybe
As it might be placed in reverence and tact

If I squint I see a sleeping earthling
With the hand of God laid thereon with cause
Has she taken the soul or just watching
Over this poor creature wrapped in gauze

The hand has so many meanings to tell
This one I would hold for ever as well

This Poet Seeks More

As we age our outer features have changed
There is nothing we can do now; yet wait,
Our nerves still feel the rush; lower I've ranged
And your breasts once suckled; now me await

Lightly; I trace my tongue around each peak
And then kiss the summits; I plant my flag
Declare these my conquests; but more I seek
Still, the softness temps me to rest and lag

I too love the tingle; oh so special
What is this spate that's so wondrous to feel
Which now whelms up within; becomes docile
Tis part and true parcel which love will heal

I shant stop this now; that which I explore
So please forgive while this poet seeks more

This Sonnet I'll Keep

We have this strong penchant for small pleasure
Those kinds that take no effort to purvey
As when I give her new poems of measure
Far-flung are those subjects she's to survey

What a wondrous cuisinière she's become
Veggies cooked al dente by candlelight
Fresh, hot pop-overs, of those I'd succumb
We share in the cleanup, I think that's right

And we don't need urging to go somewhere
She to her oil paintings, daubing colors
While I write on the couch, my poems appear
As music wafts melodious allures

And then around noon the dogs fall asleep
Before I join them this sonnet I'll keep

THIS TIME IS RIPE

Have you ever wondered why this time born
I won't concern the odds your egg survived
That gets into matters beyond; indrawn
Suffice that I say that God has contrived

The next question I pose; what then be done
Will you descry something of great portent
As for certain your gift won't be mill–run
Thus can a poem or a poet foment

My cat has this way of looking at me
It's like she is saying; don't be silly
Of course you can be great; for I foresee
Your work herald as the modern Shelley

Perhaps this time is ripe for a poet
To rouse, engage in a rally to whit

Thus I'm Skeptic

I have been told of the body's puissance
To heal itself; yet no key was offered
That would allow me to catch its nuance
Perhaps I'll search the web to be proffered

What would delve me into this strange subject
Was no mystery; lower back pain, she said
And I of course conversed; what you'd expect
For I have been trying of love re–tread

But I digress, for this topic interests
A less tactless form of succor I'd find
Where I'll lay in bed and listen to Liszt
Then self–assured in thoughts of love unwind

I've oft pooh–poohed these cures that are mystic
Perpend them to be scams; thus I'm skeptic

Till Only One Showed

I came upon a road whitened with snow
There were three cross–country ski tracks showing
That there had been skiers recent; although
I had no thought as to where they're going

The day was full of sun and the wind light
So I trudged on mindful I had no skis
Should I walk in their tracks and spoil the sight
For I'd heard that was wrong; I'd want to please

But then from the hilltop I heard chugginged
As a tractor approached; the road private
I then surmised as the tracks were flattened
Which then made my walking that more sedate

A mile further I saw the tracks leave the road
And then wind their way till only one showed

TIS A SECRET

Then what will be whispered; what tongues will wag
How did they meet; was it college amour
Those years between; fifty–five they zigzag
With no contact until a note demure

But with ne'er an answer he did persist
For then later he'd send the Rose image
Twas bright yellow and the last he'd insist
For fall was then a come; the last assuage

But they did meet; their time alone quite short
Yet it was most pleasant and a promise
To meet once more; and here God did consort
A most urgent summons to her; such bliss

Let none surmise what may of then happened
Tis a secret; mere guessing forbidden'd

To Ask of Love

Oh I am but a fool; banish me love
Tis a poor man who trifles with Cupid
And gets a strong fist instead of a glove
So I beg you forgive who's misguided

Then let me approach once more; a true friend
Nay, more than true; no truer friend there be
Than what in truth cannot of love unbend,
Cannot amend, cannot transcend for thee

Before thy maker and mine I promise
That what little love I possess I vow
Be yours to do what in your heart's fairness
You can give to a hapless lover now

I cry from the depths of my confined heart
To ask of love you're willing to impart

To Be Betrothed to You

How can I write about this love sublime
For I have broached marriage; my heart flutters
I'm all giddy, this is wonder in rhyme
I have said it and now in poem letters

Of course we must spend time with each other
Learning those small details, but what matters
Our gage d'amour; the rest doesn't bother
For love wins and my heart pitter–patters

I will say it again, will you marry me
Thus tis said and sworn most true I attest
You may save this as an answer held free
But you know it and can seal when knownst best

I will gladly offer then my banns here
To be betrothed to you for all to hear

To Find Closure

I had one last stop to make, my trip bit
That was to see Moland in Steele County
Nearby was the Lutheran Church to visit
Where my grandma Anna lies with Ole

Uncle Earl and Aunts Ruth and Gen with Cy
Lonely graves where the grass covered their names
I wiped away dead grass and leaves thereby
And took pictures to show how death becames

Mom and Dad's ash remains mix now as lain
In the bay that fronts their cabin up north
Dad had ashes dropped from Stu Shaft's airplane
And I took Mom's by boat, then poured them forth

This ends my trip journey to find closure
So now I'll write sonnets marking rest here

To Seek Guidance

It has been of thought thus let it come forth
Have I not reached my goal of a thousand
Need I prove then some more of my sole worth
Or shall I take these poems written my stand

Others have bridged writing of poems and prose
And of note the Bard's great plays, no mere work
Shall I probe this drama, learn then from those
That have success, thus my path takes a fork

But then surely a play speaks from a book
Abridged like a movie script and condensed
And would take no greater time than I took
To write this year of poems, what was preferenced

I see now that I will have to ponder
To seek guidance from those I hold fonder

To Write From Distance

How I marvel and such wonder explore
All the facets of love which I enjoy
I know that you too share in this and more
For we are like first–time sweethearts of joy

How much alike we are; wouldst thou have thought
Those two star–crossed lovers wouldst then return
For I believe God had planned this all out
Our love to wait for we had much to learn

This then is our surprise out of the blue
How else can I explain that this happened
Some force; perhaps someday I'll get a clue
But that makes no matter for love I've penned

It could be our fate to write from distance
Not to kiss or embrace, just to romance

TO WRITE POEMS, MY LIFE

Wouldst thou allow my heart to bleed unchecked
Draining my life away; my end so cruel
To lie in pain with love fettered and vexed
Oh hear me muse, give this sonnet now fuel

Thus with vigor my poem will soar to heights
And all glories gate will open; and yes
Praising each of stanzas; given sound bites
The world will know of this poet's greatness

But should you fail me, fie; no more the bard
For I shall then languish; bled dry my all
And cast to the dung heap; poet's thus marred
Never those fair ladies I will enthrall

I must implore; nay, beg of you my muse
To write poems, my life; if not, of what use

TOM HANKS AT THE AIRPORT

Be nice I told her, there's a guest coming
Which means for you to not sleep in the chair
To use your pot in the hallway plumbing
A metaphor for your litter hardware

I've cleaned both the bathrooms, washed the mirrors
Dusted and then vacuumed all the carpets
There's not much else; I've no need of Pyrrha's
My home is now complete, no needs of twits

Then at four–thirty she came in her car
Parked in the front as I then gave a tour
Quite over whelming; did I go too far
But then it was dinner; steaks were the lure

Great was the night as we watched a movie
Tom Hanks at the airport; topsy–turvy

Too Bad This Was Dreaming

If I'm dreaming then God let me have more
For this feeling transcends what was promised
My heads spinning; I feel faint and sudor
And now surely the sheets won't have crispness

I've done a quick pull–up, twisting to look
He's still behind me there, but not in range
Now I pop my speedbrakes; heed the textbook
Hoping he'll now pass–by, missing this change

I pull–back and dive straight towards the ocean
Lower my gear to keep speed slowing
There he goes by fast in downward motion
Raising gear and closing speedbrakes crowing

I've got him now; locked my missile with tone
Too bad this was dreaming; I might have known

Too Many Traffic Fines

Perhaps if I'd explained myself better
And not done what you had called plain stupid
I would not be now in this mess either
Hey, I'm a cop, not your private cupid

Listen sis, when you asked me to help you
Scare your cheating husband, I said okay
But that didn't include cuffing him too
Because he has said I have ruined his day

His boss saw my partner make the arrest
And place handcuffs on his wrists; arms behind
So now he has told you his life is messed
And will no doubt sue me, but I don't mind

For you see there was a warrant pending
As too many traffic fines out standing

Too Soon You'll Be a Grown Dog

You're a cute one Yankee doodle dandy
Born near fourth of July, a true homespun
Golden Poodle that sounds rather randy
Did I see that roguish look there of one

You take my scraps, be they food or other
I've seen an Ant eaten along with dirt
It shant matter as small kids do bother
With mud pies and peanut butter on shirt

I'll watch you there sleeping, oh so perfect
Cutesy that was a sham for you conspire
Little tricks and feints that seem suspect
Or were you just dreaming puppy's desire

I shall recall fondly these young moments
Too soon you'll be a grown dog with dormants

Until You Climb and Descry

Have you ever set your heart on winning
Something that here–to–fore were just daydreams
When then along came the seventh inning
Where you could stretch and take stock of what deems

And so you choose; wisely one would assume
But the road gets bumpy; wrong route maybe
Still, the map says proceed; what next will loom
You are wary; you weigh options; let's see

Then all of a sudden you see what's meant
You were on the correct path all along
And those daydreams become a real event
You have won and all those doubts have been wrong

It's quite common to feel goals as a wall
Until you climb and descry; it's not that tall

VERISIMILITUDE

A western omelet with cheese, ham and toast
A full meal to enjoy writing some poems
This is really delicious and I boast
Finest omelet in the egg seriatim's

Perhaps I shouldn't commit myself so
After all I have years to live and feast
And I have known Eggs Benedict, ergo
I shall retract my praise, but not of least

My thoughts are now of you flying northwest
Do they give you peanuts or just water
And does Tiki like the window seat best
Offered a pillow; no, well they oughter

I can write this sonnet about my food
Or your flight with verisimilitude

Virtues That You Now Bear as Worn

There is something about that song I hear
Is the plaintive sound to remind of poems
Of those that did suffer; early in year
When cold winter winds blew straight through sod homes

On the prairie those huge Bison they'd see
And then wonder if food would be ample
And wood for fire, perhaps deer and fowl be
Hung in sod caves from time–to–time sample

For those long hours with just candles to light
You'd tell of your growing up in Norway
To your son and daughter into the night
Until when heads laid down and slept till day

This the hardy stock of which you were born
Become virtues that you now bear as worn

Vivid My Sight

Murky morning; was it then gauze lain 'ed
As trees barely à vue hidden, orphic
And in stillness there, snow as if painted
Had God brushed on canvas gesso–morphic

Should I apply a splash of red, like rose
Letting my eyes painting appear garish
Yet this lifts the mood to joy I suppose
My own cliché as if flashy my wish

Some may think this picture portrays our lives
That we go through life with obscure features
Until a sharp event occurs; as pricked by knives
To change sudden; brightening of our futures

In an instant the scene changes with light
The sun appears and now vivid my sight

WARM MY BACK, THIS I BID

I stood and watched the sun slowly setting
A last glow; don't leave me alone I cried
Then in blues and purples the sky letting
Night fall settle I ask; has the sun died

As an early man I'd wonder this lack
Would the light appear; such worry I'd be
Then time after time the sun did come back
But then why from that side the sun I'd see

Was it playing tricks; well maybe I thought
But then I soon tired of thinking about
As more pressing events; would fish be caught
And a place to sleep; then a smile came out

There was the sun again; fooled me you did
But stay awhile, warm my back; this I bid

We and Two Gals

I sat talking with friend Richard of things
That was nibbling away in our cached thoughts
Both of us past the three quarter mark brings
Recall of our growing up; the saved spots

But we're different as one rightly suspects
His large history with scores of close family
While my own is small, not what one expects
Of a Norseman, but then some were soli

Both of us plan trips north to our home towns
His near Windy City, full of toll roads
Mine to Fairbo, the chic title unwounds
Within my head; my trip how well it bodes

It was quiet today, few to abide
We and two gals playing scrabble outside

We Have This Chance but Once

Ask me and I'll tell you; honest I'll be
For I'm truly blessed in meeting again
My love of past years; her vision I see
Is most wondrous; this love of mine most fain

God has looked down and said; perhaps this pair
Deserves another chance of love, of Eden
That here is a story; shall I prepare
Those to write of it or will it just lend

Now I am not one to cross swords with God
Offered, I take this then as a command
And will do my utmost to more than nod
I'll put all my passion towards this end

Join thus with me; partner love à jamais
We have this chance but once; God's given we

WE TASTE OF LOVE DELIGHT

Let me love you complete, promised I plight
And in return a soft hello suffice
Let me care and protect throughout the night
Knowing that I'm there, your whispers so nice

Let me feed you morsels, finest entrée
Then pick the wine replete, your choice given
Let me drink of beauty, there now I'll pay
It's been my own pleasure, your smile even

Let me guide you, strolling our way homeward
Rest your arm there, fastened we are in love
Let me bring you to your doorstep, awkward
I face you now, you look, will he ask of

Let me kiss you, your lips do so invite
And with embrace we taste of love delight

WE'LL DO IT ONCE AGAIN

We made the fire dance; our first nights outing
I searched for wood and found small limbs and bark
Then my Karen poked the embers to sing
This so wondrous as we sat in the dark

Then a whistle announced the trains return
Twas the dinner special to the Cumbres
Like a zephyr; it's sound the night's nocturne
Winding its way; showing us its nightdress

As the darkness settled over our fire
Only sparks and embers remained of heat
Then with much wine I'm now quick to admire
And I'll say to Karen; Hon it's a treat

It's been a day; a most wondrous heyday
We'll do it once again and say; hurray

What If this Poem Were Lewd

I'm tired, weary, fatigued, jaded and fagged
Other that those I'm fine; did I say ouch
So when I walked into the H. B. D.
And saw this huge white dog, memories debauch

She was like a huge cloud and named Powder
And the heat may have caused her to drool here
So I asked her owner, does heat bother
It's her age that matters, now though not ere

I paused in thought, recalled then a white dog
Surely more than one lives nearby my place
That it might have been a sign, I'm agog
Did it occur by chance, a slight efface

I should never write when I'm in this mood
My mind wanders; what if this poem were lewd

WHAT IS ONE MORE HILL

You have opened my heart to love again
And I made a mistake rushing things through
So let me show resolve as I begin
Courtship of a lasting purpose with you

It may have been caprice to think marriage
For I now know I have pursued a dream
Which could only then be hard to manage
As I was drawn (too fast) to the cream

I have given sanction of a desire
To love you most fully as a compeer
Which means I will support; never to tire
As a spouse–in–waiting; remain most dear

I have loved you for a very long time
What is one more hill that I need to climb

What Lies Beyond the Bend

My love, my love must you leave me wanting
Hold me tightly I can't bear you to leave
Kiss me; kiss me your lips now so haunting
Will you write me sending poems of reprieve

Hold me, hold me Mother, my pain doth start
And it hurts me badly when I think how
Like an arrow this news has pierced my heart
For he'll not know the child within me now

Pray thee, pray thee dear Lord that I survive
This most restive battle, at one's wits' end
For we suffer the gas and shells arrive
Never knowing what lies beyond the bend

Oh my darling tis you only I miss
Keep me, keep me safely from this chaos

What My Heart is Telling

I would believe you were born a damsel
Daughter of the Duke and Duchess of Meath
There you caught me glimpsing; your hair hazel;
The light color glistens; your face beneath

I would believe you came from the Far East
Mixture of an Aussie and a Brit nurse
Beauty eludes although my eyes did feast
Of your body; all in good taste and terse

I would believe you came as you told me
Honest and then forthright; no punches pulled
I have known from the get–go I'd foresee
That you my dear would add to life most full'd

I shall believe what my heart is telling
That I love you Karen where you're dwelling

What Vapor Now Comes My Way

Let me breathe, what vapor now comes my way
Tis Her essence that I inhale; thus stung
I greet this sweetened air that smells of Rosebay,
Tea and Honeysuckle that tangs my tongue

Now She comes; a vesper, my evening star
Always to be the first to greet my eye
As She nears, I see no footprints to mar
The dew that lays glistened, for She doth fly

I'll watch Her until my lids start to close
And soon my breathing becomes like the wind
And darkness enfolds me; Her arms have chose
To hold me through the night; my life destined

And as dawn breaks; my morning star; Venus
Greets me, then winks as She'd known my purpose

When All Is At Peace

When all is at peace and snuggled in bed
And the Fairies cavort and Sprites lay forth
Then bring you dreams of far away, I've said
For you are most precious of all things worth

Look down and see gardens of lush pleasure
There the Camels drink their fill of water
Before they cross hot sands, the sky azure
But you are cool as you fly much farther

Then now below, see the Lions stalking
That small herd of Gnus, oh what a strange name
And there in the grass tall men with spears walking
Tending cattle watching out for wild game

The sun now is rising, your sleep ending
You stir, hugging the stuffed Lion tending

WHEN IN DREAMS

Moonlight streaming through my open window
And I'm awake thinking about you there
Is the moon's light bathing as on tip–toe
Not to make you stir but somehow aware

If you could look now you'd see my features
They are mirrored in the lunar surface
See now, I'm not frowning, nor be creatures
To haunt you there for I'm sending a kiss

A cloud has passed over hiding the moon
But that shouldn't concern you there sleeping
Perhaps you've turned over; the dawn comes soon
And you'll waken and see my face peeping

I'd give of life to then capture moonbeams
For I'd strew them over you when in dreams

When My Love Comes to Me

Tis your voice that on morning wakens me
Softer than the White Winged Dove's plaintive coo
More melic than the Kingbird's euphony
There to resonate within my heart too

I am on the wind, floating; you command
Then in the stream that winds within your soul
I be tunneled deep, ne'er dislodge, disband
But held fast as was I to buttonhole

Then let me be around as night comes on
For then the words that I hear will lull me
To slumber in ecstasy for anon
In my dreams I'll savor them vis–à–vis

Tis a joyful note that I hear each day
When my love comes to me by what she'd say

WHEN MY LOVES NEAR ME

Is it true that poets write best when sad
One might well think that its possibly true
On the other hand I write best when glad
And my temper is more joyful hereto

So then why this spate, this rush of anger
It does nothing but to bitter the well
One would hope this feeling might well languor
Thus to subside; become then more tranquil

Perhaps it is the mood one feels instead
Like the music writer who pens his song
In key major or minor it is led
By his feelings at that moment how strong

One things certain and that is I write best
When my loves near me and I'm not depressed

WHEN ONE PAINT WITH PURPLE

Who came in and sprayed the purple color
Was it you for there's paint around your eye
And in your hair, do you feel of dolor
Or was it just a whim, Blue Berry Pie

Bring me Michael and Jell–O for my paint
Grape would be fine; matching the mess he's made
A self portrait done with mirror he shan't
As he is no lefty of paint fame paid

One must wonder of what he was painting
I know I said a self portrait; his own
But that was said to fool you there waiting
A nude descending in a purple nightgown

When one paint with purple expect what's meant
That it be the hue worn as King's garment

When Sleep Comes to You

Let me hold your hand; nay don't pull away
But stick with me for just these few moments
I have something to ask of you today
It has welled up; I can't contain silence

Please look at me; I must see your eyes now
For they will tell me truth before goodbyes
I love you; oh I must tell you somehow
Yet it's hard to utter, but I shall try

I leave when the sun wakes, to go to fight
And I reckon my chance to live is nil
Then take my ring as a promise tonight
That I should wed thee love wouldst time standstill

I'll hold you strong within my arms till morn
Then when sleep comes to you I'll leave; withdrawn

WHEN THE ENDING A BIT FINER

A poet's life should end with a sonnet
With its meter and rhyme; structured and form
I'd make it pretty; liken'd Easter bonnet
Full of colors and frills that I'd adorn

Nothing harmful in it would cause alarm
Just a lasting lament from the mimic
Showing his stuff; how great poems ne'er do harm
That would be self–defeating, cause panic

No, a simple epitaph; that's all
Here lies the poet; you'd thought he'd know'd it
But then again perhaps he'd dropped the ball
And really wanted a lewd limerick

In the end he'd settle for one–liner
All's well when the ending a bit finer

Where Whey From Cheese Poured Out

They have outside seating but the wind cold
So I sit now inside at a window
This looks east towards sandstone like gold
Do they know of caves we'd explored below

Kenny Sexter was a station knower
A friend of dads, I'd watch the trains resting
While the water poured from water tower
And steam would shoot; poosih, pooish misting

Sometimes when I was of hurry I'd climb
Between the trains carriage, but that was wrong
And the train's men would yell; you'll lose your limb
But I'd scatter up the Ravine Street long

Carp fish would swim where whey from cheese poured out
The straight River foul, we'd soon learn about

Will My Passion Subside

I've come again into your world surround
And I'm not sure that I'm wanted therein
Should I just leave, vanish not be around
Would that please you or would heartache begin

I tried to stay away; god knows how well
And it is just inane; that is so true
But my heart still rules, thumps aloud to tell
My soul, carry on you fool, you'll subdue

Who made my heart fervent for it glows hot
So much so that cooling by cold showers
Only warms the water, heartened, it's not
Perhaps I'll lie within the cool bowers

These things all now happen as I'm eighteen
Will my passion subside when I'm nineteen

WILL-O'-THE-WISP

Will-o'-the-wisp you say now in jest Sir
I don't agree, well you knew that of course
For I intend marriage, of that I'm sure
I have her heart, let the family remorse

My son, really now, how little you know
These are royal stock, they marry among
So your chances are nil, forget her now
Or else feel the pain, their arrows have stung

But I cannot accede, their law be damned
She loves me, oh truly I tell to thee
Then see tonight at the chapel we've planned
Marriage vows to be blessed by the priest we

Those in love wear blinders, they see not clear
Often then fate befalls shedding of tear

With Fancy Comes Verve

Then let there be merry blithesome spirit
You who dances upon my pen ad hoc
Shall I write a sonnet sweet with skirret
Fried with fresh brought morels, peas and ham hock

Thrill me with your twirling while I compose
A fixed verse of meter teasing with rhyme
Let the world hear laughter as it bellows
Festive with sounds; simple tunes and ragtime

Then go flutter away and leave me be
As deep thoughts are required for this writing
A poem of such beauty penned here for thee
Of love given free and ne'er be slighting

Thus be it writ that with fancy comes verve
And with sonnets the warmth that thou deserve

WITH HONEST LOVE

It shall never be; this love I pursue
Yet I shall strive hardest with all my might
Time and then time again she's said; adieu
Still, the flame burns; foolish I did ignite

Thus my credo; I shall never give up
Even if she reproves what I advance
I swear to her that this is no cock–up
Like the shy lad, I will ask her to dance

Oh my sweet, my love; you I do adore
I'm Romeo to you my Juliet
I'd climb to your window, there to implore
You to receive sonnets from this poet

In your heart you know that I do revere
You with honest love; of that I'm sincere

WITH PAIN TO CEASE

Of late my poems protract love gone astray
Is it in my mind that only I see
To then battle wits which seek to allay
My heart and mind at cross purpose they be

It is fancy I know, not what I feel
Stubborn, no more mulish this quest of mine
What I seek is pardon for what was real
If not that then forgive what acts entwine

Perhaps the gods laugh at bêtise thus shown
Amidst yucks and yowls their glee I suffer
Poor this mortal whose broken heart now known
Let him dangle to show a fools offer

At the end of this road I may find peace
Letting me to return with pain to cease

With This Fine Woman

I've pulled the space heater closer to me
Bundled up, I need the warmth of springtime
And not the chill that now invades my knee
Maybe I should have worn leggings meantime

Yes, the heat is of much comfort writing
At least the ink flows quite freely this morn
Now if only my lines too were brightening
I would then feel better and not forlorn

For you see, I miss my lady Karen
She is away in far Phoenix city
And I find my visions of life barren;
Her warmth I miss; snuggled close and pretty

Being as a poet is quite common
Yet it livens up with this fine woman

WITHIN BEDROOM WALLS TO STUFFED TOYS

Tell me Bear what do you think of Stephen
He's asked me to be his steady with ring
I like him, well a lot I guess, but then
What should I do about Frank; not a thing

You nod your head, is that a yes you mean
Then I shall tell Stephen that I accept
And won't Jo and Nancy just hope I'm seen
Walking the halls, the ring swung on chain kept

My sweet little Bear I tell you so much
Promise you'll not breathe a word of that's told
You must give your word, my secrets as such
Are just between us two, my wishes so bold

What young, and some not so young, have confessed
Within bedroom walls to stuffed toys is guessed

WOMAN OF DREAMS

When I write of love I think of you Anne
Then it is quite easy to pen my poems
I let my hand have free reign and then man
The words and phrases pour out like waves and foams

Am I then a genius; hardly I think
Just a natural talent; giving zingers
Like; the breeze wafts cool, then whispers; soft Mink
The feel; her hair running through my fingers

I could write a thousand lines of rhymed verse
And still have more for my sonnets of love
For no matter how I tell it my purse
Has an ample supply; there's no end of

Write on them my poet; sonnets, whole reams
Let love come forth; my Anne; woman of dreams

Wouldst I Tell of More

We're like two ships steaming along abreast
Loath that we touch yet still wanting closeness
To be within hailing distance insist
Should a peril occur we'd have nearness

Like the Jonquil which in springtime erupts
White and yellow flowers saying we're here
So too shall our love then spring forth from depths
Of cold winters, of a malaise we bear

Pretend as a baby Rabbit you're held
Such soft fur and pink tinged ears I'm petting
Cuddled within my hands, yet soon I yield
To your warm nest I place now safe setting

All these figures of speech speak of love yearned
Wouldst I tell of more, but lines too few turned

WOULDST I THEN RUE

Tonight I have put forth sonnets trio
And so at last, but not certain the least
I could choose to start a novel bio
The life and time of I, ah such a beast

It would have to be of import smitten
And my poems could be the kernel needed
How I had thus blossomed as poems written
Become then an author, my works deeded

I'm too toying with a plot that explains
What few of the poems mean, their purport
Expand these as subplots within the mains
That of telling of truths and fond support

What a job this becomes if I pursue
And of at least a year, wouldst I then rue

Wouldst the Brook Still Hear

I feel the sound building within me now
Climbing to its climax my heart beats fast
There, there, it just pulsates; wouldst I allow
This great music to change me; make it last

These songs elude; my thirst cries for succor
Then I hear the tenor sing from Bohéme
And I am once again sufficed with more
I am sated; there is no end to blame

Does the timbre of these tones now resound
For I hear the refrain over again
Much like the loud Anvil Chorus which pound
Its beat constant; my poems here which have lain

Should my voice be stilled where music's absent
Wouldst the brook still hear its gurgle present

WRITE OUT MY SENT EMAILS

I write my poems in long hand or cursive
In one–hundred page bound notebooks before
I type them in Word, print them out and give
The poems a last read through for errs I pore

These I should seal and mail then back to me
Make me then sign for the package and not open
To be proof that I wrote these poems you see
Authors do this, proof that they had written

I should like to write you only by pen
But since email is much quicker I bend
To our modern ways of sending them then
But in secret I will write out and send

I have these notes that I will use shortly
Write out my sent emails, done thus smartly

WRITING POEMS OF LOVE'S BLISS

How must I then convey my love; to gush
For in simple language the words shant flow
Yet in those same words did romance flourish
In years now long past, loves guileless did know

Use of facial or of body gestures
Would I suppose suffice; then what of prose
Must I forsake my poem, poet's nurtures
That thrills the heart whence read at nights compose

For you see love, my heart and soul in poem
Is the descant I feel so warm inside
I'm no actor or mime; words are my home
Where I craft love sonnets of which much pride

I have come the complete circle in this
Back to my mien, writing poems of love's bliss

Years Had Not Bode He

How can I make sense of that which happened
To a young man madly in love long past
I might try but likely would fail rended
In small pieces never again to last

Suppose then this fellow wished not sully
This Norse princess yet in yearning felt so
Helpless, so torn with loves rapture fully
That in toto he did in fact do woe

I might rate his charm plus but sense minus
He was nineteen, a lad still wet in ears
That a complex affair would fool him thus
I must agree, his mind not yet in years

Let it lay bare this love which longed to be
Tis best to say that years had not bode he

Yet Grow Amorous in Strength

When I sit up in bed writing at night
Will you wonder what my sonnets about
Shall you peek, see a line; you have that right
So don't you be afraid my love cries out

I write these lines; they are floating, wafting
Do you see them approach; enfolding you here
Swirling around, gently; almost laughing
They bring forth my joy and comfort most dear

Oh, I will let you read each one written
For it sends thrills within me; each comment
Those oohs and ahhs just tell that you're smitten
And that my time will spent; cosmic moment

By now you are resting, touching my length
I am content; yet grow amorous in strength

YET I TRY

Should I of love compare of thee forthwith
By what milestone doth one judge most fairly
Where in truth I expound, ne'er would I rift
As I view her splendid, what more dare be

The love I feel transcends that of passion
It most marvels, one feels, of long rapture
That which enthralls; never out of fashion
Like the wave, the highest crest to capture

Be still my heart, let me love her with care
And not make of demands which are empty
Rather with true kindness let me then share
In her dreams and hopes; my honored duty

Few words I write express my heart felt love
Yet I try with all my strength made hereof

Yet the Leaves Still Flutter

Over my head is heard rustle of leaves
The light wind now wafting gently blowing
As I rest here docile, my mind at ease
Then lets me view her face, oft where glowing

I'm shook awake; Sire, you are now needed
Very well Shaun, give me my best breastplate
Then go saddle Rogan and drape him red
I'll take hammer and my long sword as mate

Declan are the archers set to barrage
And our men, each with a weapon request
I'll ride the ranks stirring them up with rage
Then on signal start your march to conquest

All his thoughts now of the battle to see
Yet the leaves still flutter, not stilled they be

You Are Wanted On Set

I must say you look like hell this morning
Twas a happy night, no; I jest of course
For I see in your eyes tears of mourning
Perhaps of fright too if that could be worse

Go see now your dentist; your teeth ghastly
And while in town, do you require glasses
I'd much prefer tinted ones; and lastly
You need hair, wouldst Afro style give passes

You have a face only mother could love
Well me too in a way, special you see
As there's plenty of those horror shots of
Zombies chasing young girls; you're some body

Hold on now, I hear the phone start ringing
You are wanted on set, tumult bringing

You Ask What a Poet Thinks

You ask what a poet thinks when he writes
How just the right phrases seem to appear
That I answer; know not what thought alights
It must precede my pen moving my dear

Be it music that sets the mood this poem
Perhaps as I float in songs of romance
A tune excites some cell within my dome
Their small flashes causing atoms to dance

Then it might be I put me tout à fait
As I wear the skin of some love struck teen
And I can see what must happen; foresee
And put thereto her words as then is seen

I don't believe even for an instant
That Will Shakespeare borne in me as infant

You Get What You Want

Maybe she was correct; I'll find someone
I must admit I have not been active
One does not go helter–skelter; not done
It just happens; don't look for a motive

Then my plan is no plan; that is simple
Just go about business as per usual
And don't look for any magic portal
Stay calm and let fate work itself gradual

Think back on how you met all your women
It was by some mishap; something not planned
There you were and no one fired a cannon
You looked up and there she was; all suntanned

Patience is a virtue that is called for
You get what you want by having rapport

You Have My Love

I have poured out all that my heart contains
So you now know secrets here–to–for borne
That this cleansing allows what then pertains
Of those privy, a blank image forlorn

I now begin with a clean heart unspoiled
That we can store our love safely ever
And not bewray this trust given, not roiled
By false starts and endings; priors aver

That you know my heart, art thou now bemused
And can revel in the smallest of sins
You have captured and now possess what used
To be my soul, truly this is of wins

What take of this; empty I have no guess
You have my love stolen I now confess

You May as Well Flirt

From the dust of this planet comes greatness
See it swirling around; you must catch it
Then mold it in your mind; just be fearless
And take a chance; you'll be surprised poet

Telling of a journey, voicing a yarn
Relating a truth spoken divine by right
Then in duple meter write your pavane
Be it a dirge or a lovesick good–night

In tones of sheer glory tell your story
And do not be afraid; ill–used grammar
Is right on and you needn't be sorry
You're the author, shout it out; clamor

From the lint, the ash, the powder and dirt
Craft your poems with love; you may as well flirt

You Never Adjure

There is this sound I hear; silent to you
Are you being coy, for really it's loud
And I was now thinking about, if true
Might I want to hum the song; I'd be proud

Sometimes it's a prelude; opening my heart
Making the start of my day so special
Other times I hear a brass band depart
The rat–tat–tat of a drummer's jovial

Then at night when whispers become our norm
I hear duets of love; dulcet to taste
And I say so softly; we are reborn
Hear the music of such rapport embraced

In time you will hear these sounds of amour
And then wonder why you never adjure

You Showed Me No Face

You came into my dream; I was waiting
And there you were, nothing had changed at all
We talked of love and who we were dating
I thought this is nice here getting the call

Then just like that you were gone from my sight
I guess I had figured you had vanished
And it wasn't too long before my night
Had run its course and I awoke famished

Throughout the day I thought about the dream
Was there then a message, something you said
But I couldn't think at all, 'twere no gleam
Of facts salient to a past love gone bad

And now later I still wonder of you
You showed me no face, if not thou, then who

YOUR CALM REPLY OF LOVE

I do safeguard that you not lose of love
For I find my last poem written with rue
Binding my heart tight, not letting go of
Being with you more than just that once view

So let me quell our fears; remain as were
Dreaming of such wondrous thoughts each other
And to let the wind take us with its air
To a place not known but which we savor

There's no reason I should be glum this night
Your note gives me rapture and much delight
I find no code hidden between your write
Is this then the poet looking less bright

My mind is now betwixt poems above
I shall await your calm reply of love

YOUR SAFE REFUGE

Your love is a strength that holds me steady
When just the right word is needed you speak
And when I'm in pain your help is ready
To ease my doubts; you aid me when I'm weak

I ask myself of what manner can one
Repay this love for now surely I must
Thus be I a pillar of force; weakened by none
That will always protect you as is just

I want you to be gay, to be happy
To live life just knowing I'm here always
To aid you should my help along the way
Be of service to see you through life's haze

I am your rock, your firm, holdfast anchor
Your safe refuge, you bloom should you languor

You're a Working Dog

Welcome Nikki, you're a gorgeous canine
Light brown with mottled spots what is your age
Thirteen, why I wouldn't have guessed past nine
You're a cattle dog with knowledge most sage

I have noticed your ears upright, listening
Is it Sparrows you hear chirping for food
Just a tiny mouthful, they perch resting
Then bored, you plop down, life really is good

Time to get up, you sense movement to go
But first a drink of cool water from pail
Nice of Happy Belly Deli to know
That dog too gets thirsty wagging their tail

You've got a leash and a tag so legal
You're a working dog and not a Beagle

404   Stanley Paul Thompson

About the Author

Stanley Thompson has continued writing poetry since the publication of his book, *Sonnets of Life Well Spent*. Of his now nearly 3500 poems written, 850 are newly written sonnets, and it is from these that he has selected 400 for this tome.

A retired Naval Officer and pilot of carrier jet aircraft, he received his Master's degree in Meteorology at the United States Naval Postgraduate School in Monterey, California. He has taught college mathematics, statistics, oceanography, and naval history at four separate universities.

Nonetheless a late entry into the field of poetry, he has embraced it fully, writing sonnets, pentameter verse, and in meter and rhyme of Keats, Shelley and Lord Byron. In an unnamed ode (yet unpublished) he has written about a fictional figure of Norse descent (he is of Norwegian blood) that chronicles his own heritage. This ode is of 173 stanza of eight line rhyming verse.

He continues his life writing poems about everyday events; traveling the country in an aged Winnebago Mini RV, visiting coffee cafés and bookstores, watching trains (an activity that his wife has encouraged), gardening, observing birds and animals, and his many volunteer activities.

Mr. Thompson resides in Southern New Mexico.

Made in the USA
San Bernardino, CA
18 October 2014